This volume was donated to SAIPAR
by the Michigan State University
African Studies Center
and its Associated Faculty

**SOCIAL CHANGE AND
IMAGES OF THE FUTURE**

INTERNATIONAL STUDIES IN POLITICAL AND SOCIAL CHANGE

Series Editor: WENDELL BELL, Yale University

1. The Democratic Revolution in the West Indies: Studies in Nationalism, Leadership, and the Belief in Progress
   edited by Wendell Bell

2. The Sociology of Political Independence: A Study of Nationalist Attitudes Among West Indian Leaders
   by Charles C. Moskos, Jr.

3. Black Intellectuals Come to Power: The Rise of Creole Nationalism in Trinidad & Tobago
   by Ivar Oxaal

4. Social Change and Images of the Future: A Study of the Pursuit of Progress in Jamaica
   by James A. Mau

A STUDY OF THE PURSUIT
OF PROGRESS IN JAMAICA

Social Change and Images of The Future

James A. Mau
Yale University

SCHENKMAN PUBLISHING COMPANY, Inc.
CAMBRIDGE, MASSACHUSETTS

Copyright © 1968

SCHENKMAN PUBLISHING COMPANY, INC.
Cambridge, Massachusetts 02138

PRINTED IN THE UNITED STATES OF AMERICA

All rights reserved. This book, or parts thereof, may not be reproduced in any form without written permission of the publishers.

Library of Congress Catalog Card Number: 67-29327

For Gail, Matthew, and Michael

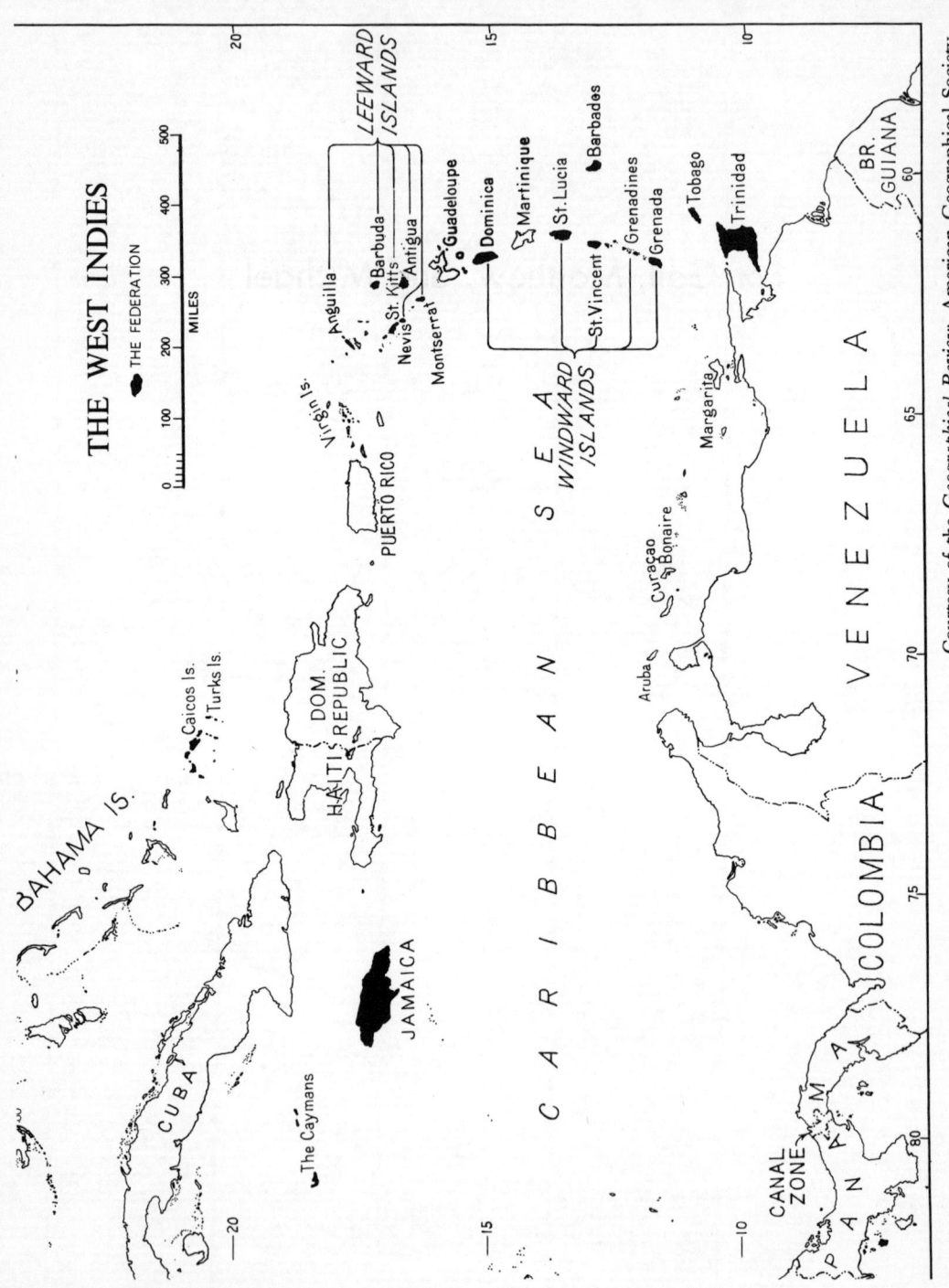
Courtesy of the *Geographical Review*, American Geographical Society.

Editor's Note

The forces of nationalism provide the background for this sociological study of images of a new nation's future. Professor Mau reports on the ideologies of key leaders in the island of Jamaica just prior to its political independence in August, 1962. He examines leaders' attitudes towards change, probes their views of the future, and shows the importance of such views in shaping the emerging future of the nation. He seeks the answers to these questions: Why do some leaders believe in progress? Why do others reject the belief in progress and have fatalistic and self-damning expectations for the future? How do such beliefs affect the emerging future itself?

Additionally, Professor Mau's study is distinctive in its design in that it permits a comparison of differential images of the future held by elites and masses as well as an evaluation of the reciprocal images of each group held by the other. Professor Mau compares the amount of hostility attributed to the urban lower socio-economic-racial classes by leaders to their actual hostility as determined from interviews with such lower-class persons themselves. The results are somewhat surprising, and the author uses them to show how the "tragic circle of fear, social disaster, and reinforced fear might be broken."

The discussion and conclusions are based on data collected in interviews with national leaders as well as with a sample of persons living in a lower-class shack town in the West side of Kingston, Jamaica's major city. The plight of the urban lower classes — about 100,000 people in Western Kingston — was both symbol and substance of one of the most important social problems facing the soon-to-be independent country. Its solution was — and is — of crucial relevance to the success of the new national leaders as they come to power.

This volume is the fourth in a new series of "International Studies in Political and Social Change." Like the first three volumes, it contains a report of research done as part of the U.C.L.A. West Indies Study Program during the early 1960's. With its publication, the major results of the Program are complete.

WENDELL BELL

Acknowledgements

The primary financial support for this research came from the Social Science Research Council which granted me a pre-doctoral fellowship during the years 1961–63; and from the West Indies Studies Program of the University of California, Los Angeles which was financed by the Carnegie Corporation of New York, and directed by Wendell Bell. I was a Fellow in this program during the years 1960–63. In addition, funds for travel and expenses in Jamaica were provided by the Concilium on International Studies of Yale University. I also thank Yale University for a Junior Faculty Fellowship in 1966–67, during which the final editing of this manuscript was completed.

Sufficient thanks to Wendell Bell for his continued guidance, counsel, criticism, and friendship cannot be expressed in few words here. I can only hope that some of his commitment to scholarship and humanity and its impression on me can be found in my own work. My debt to him is indeed great. And to Lora-Lee Bell I offer my deepest thanks for her continued helpfulness especially during fieldwork in Jamaica.

I should also like to thank the other Fellows of the West Indies Study Program for their time and help in many discussions of this research. They are Andrew G. J. Comacho, James T. Duke, Neville W. Layne, Anthony P. Maingot, Charles C. Moskos, Jr., Ivar Oxaal, Dudley E. Parris, and Andrew P. Phillips. Also for many helpful criticisms and suggestions, I thank Professors Walter E. Freeman, George A. Huaco, Leo Kuper, Joseph La Palombara, Raymond W. Mack, Raymond J. Murphy, Michael G. Smith, and Richard C. Snyder.

Special thanks are due the many people in Jamaica without whose assistance, advice, friendship, and cooperation this research would have been exceedingly more difficult, if not impossible. Their warm hospitality often made me feel more like a Jamaican than just another transient scholar. Particularly, I wish to thank Dr. H. D. Huggins, former Director of the Institute of Social and Economic Research at the University of the West Indies, Jamaica, and the faculty and staff of the Institute for their helpful advice and hospitality; and also the officers and staff of the former Jamaica Social Welfare Commission for their support and cooperation.

For many hours of serious conversation and friendly fieldwork experiences I should like to offer special thanks to Mr. and Mrs. Vernon L. Arnett, Mr. and Mrs. J. D. Barnes, and Mr. Hector Gibson, and their families. Their interest and help are truly appreciated.

An earlier version of Chapter 8 was published before, and is included here in a revised and expanded version. For permission to use this material, I wish to thank Fuat Andic and Thomas Mathews, Editors of *The Caribbean in Transition: Papers on Social, Political, and Economic Development*, Río Piedras, Puerto Rico: Institute of Caribbean Studies, 1965.

For many hours of typing and other assistance, I thank Carol Cofrancesco, Nora Quiocho, Lorraine Estra, Priscilla Baxter, Cathy Ralston, and Patricia Ledbetter of Yale University. I am grateful to Janet G. Turk for preparing the index and proofreading.

Finally, I thank my wife Gail, who has endured the whole experience with good humor, and who typed and retyped continually without complaint as the manuscript grew and I became more unbearable.

New Haven, Connecticut JAMES A. MAU
October, 1967

Contents

Editor's Note		vii
Acknowledgements		ix
Chapter One	Introduction	1
Chapter Two	Jamaica: Yesterday and Today	14
Chapter Three	Images of the Future	36
Chapter Four	An Index of Belief in Progress	57
Chapter Five	Equality and Belief in Progress	66
Chapter Six	Power and Belief in Progress	79
Chapter Seven	Knowledge and Belief in Progress	88
Chapter Eight	The Myth of the Hostile Masses	98
Chapter Nine	Conclusion	113
Appendix One	Field Work and Study Design	118
Appendix Two	Index Construction	130
Appendix Three	Interview Schedule — Jamaican Leaders	138
Indexes		141

List of Tables

1. Annual increases in Gross National Product: 1953–1962 — 22
2. National income per capita, 1955–1962 — 22
3. Percentage contribution of selected industrial sectors to Gross Domestic Product at factor cost, 1938–1962 — 23
4. Percentage distribution of farms by size and acreage in each size group, 1954 and 1961 — 25
5. Percentage distribution of Jamaican leaders according to their responses to four questions about the future — 37
6. Percentage distribution of Jamaican leaders and urban lower-class respondents according to their images of the future, expected effects of independence, and evaluation of past change — 46
7. International comparisons of past, present, future evaluations — 49
8. Scale criteria related to the index of belief in progress — 59
9. Percentage distribution of Jamaican leaders according to scale scores on the index of belief in progress — 60
10. Percentage of Jamaican leaders who favorably evaluated past change by belief in progress — 61
11. Percentage of Jamaican leaders who believe in progress by selected social characteristics — 63
12. Percentage of Jamaican leaders who believe in progress by type of elite position — 64
13. Percentage of Jamaican leaders who are egalitarians — 68
14. Percentage of Jamaican leaders who are egalitarians by selected social characterics — 72
15. Percentage of Jamaican leaders who are egalitarians by type of elite position — 74
16. Percentage of Jamaican leaders who believe in progress by attitudes toward equality — 75
17. Percentage of Jamaican leaders who are most powerful by selected social characteristics — 83
18. Percentage of Jamaican leaders who are most powerful by type of elite position — 84
19. Percentage of Jamaican leaders who believe in progress by the index of power — 85
20. Percentage of Jamaican leaders who believe in progress by attitudes toward equality and the index of power — 86
21. Percentage of Jamaican leaders who are most knowledgeable by selected social characteristics — 91
22. Percentage of Jamaican leaders who are most knowledgeable by type of elite position — 92

23. Percentage of Jamaican leaders who believe in progress by the index of knowledge 93
24. Percentage of Jamaican leaders who believe in progress by the index of knowledge and attitudes toward equality 95
25. Percentage of Jamaican leaders who believe in progress by the index of knowledge and the index of power 95
26. Percentage of Jamaican leaders who believe in progress by the composite index of egalitarianism, power, and knowledge 96
27. Percentage of Jamaican leaders who believe in progress by perceived attitudes of urban lower class toward the upper and middle classes 104
28. Percentage of Jamaican leaders who perceive the urban lower classes to be hostile by egalitarianism 105
29. Percentage of Jamaican leaders who perceive the urban lower classes to be hostile by the index of power 106
30. Percentage of Jamaican leaders who perceive the urban lower classes to be hostile by index of knowledge 106
31. Percentage of Jamaican leaders who perceive the urban lower classes to be hostile by the composite index of egalitarianism, power, and knowledge 107
32. Percentage of urban lower-class respondents who believe in progress by level of political mobilization 110

CHAPTER 1 Introduction

Once upon a time a sociologist had twin sons. One was a confirmed pessimist, and the other was a complete optimist. Their father was somewhat alarmed and puzzled by this and decided to try an experiment. On their birthday he filled the pessimist's room with everything a little boy could wish for, and he filled the optimist's room with piles of hay. The next morning he watched their reactions to their situations. The pessimist sat slumped among the games, toys, and other playthings, eyeing the presents with suspicion and wondering what was going on. His puzzled father walked to the other boy's room, and discovered him standing waist deep in the hay, digging through it and laughing joyously. The father said, "Son, what are you doing? What are you so happy about?" Still laughing, the boy turned to his dad saying, "Jeez, Dad, with all this hay here, there must be a pony!"

In simple terms, the question addressed in this study is somewhat like that confronting the puzzled father in this story. Why did some Jamaicans, when thinking about the present situation of their nation at the time of political independence and about its history, have only dreadful expectations and dire predictions about the future of the new nation and its people; and why did others have equally firm beliefs that the future of the nation would be most favorable, that the desired social, economic, and political changes which had recently begun would continue, that the most appropriate image of the future of the new nation was one of increasing progress? At the one extreme, why did some anticipate continued or greater poverty, misfortune, and violence in Jamaica, and others affirm that the nation's future would be better than ever before? Why did some of the Jamaicans studied believe in the likelihood of progress for Jamaica and its people, and others negate these beliefs? These questions concerning the belief in progress in the island-nation of Jamaica during the final stages of its transition to political independence constitute the core subject of this research.

The idea of progress was one of the dominant themes of the democratic revolution which began in Jamaica in the late 1930's. Since then Jamaica has experienced great political development, rapid economic development, and considerable technological advance. This study explores the impact of these and related changes, and other social factors on the images of the future held by Jamaicans in the months preceding their achievement of politically independent status within the British Commonwealth of nations.

THE IDEA OF PROGRESS

The idea of progress has had a mixed career in modern man's image of the future. Since its emergence in the first years of the seventeenth century, it has been variously accepted as a credo, developed as philosophy, scorned as foolish or naive, and rejected as bourgeois nonsense. Whether accepted or rejected, the idea of progress in its changing conceptions has been a dominant theme in modern intellectual history. As embodied in utopian images of the future, it has influenced social philosophy and science, socialism and sociology. Until recently, the historic impact of the idea of progress on man's images of the future has been restricted to a small proportion of the world's people. Its influence has been limited largely to the European and North American continents, while the mass of Asians, Africans, and Latin Americans have been clinging to the present or looking with hope to the golden ages of the past. Today this is no longer true. Peoples throughout the world are turning to the future with awareness, and the presently growing importance of these people to the future of the world in part lies in their images of the future, in their belief — or disbelief — in progress.

The history of the idea of progress in its modern forms is principally a part of the history of Europe since the early seventeenth century. Certainly the intellectual climate which favored the emergence of the idea of progress had been developing for a long time, but it was in the birth of the scientific revolution that the way was clearly set. "The beginnings of the movement are fittingly symbolized by a famous statement of Galileo, which suggests that he was more concerned with 'how the heavens go' than with 'how one goes to heaven'."[1]

As noted by J. B. Bury in his comprehensive study of the origin and growth of the idea of progress, we might well be surprised that the Greek scholars of classical antiquity did not develop the idea of progress as a conception of historical change.[2] Although they were quite

---

[1] Bruce Mazlish, "The Idea of Progress," *Daedalus*, 92 (Summer, 1963), 447.
[2] J. B. Bury, *The Idea of Progress*, New York: Dover Publications, Inc., 1955, p. 7; this work was first published in 1920.

clearly concerned with problems of the nature and origin of change, the Greek philosophers' formulations generally were either doctrines of degeneration from a Golden Age of the past, or statements of cycles of alternation from birth through life to death and rebirth, without any apparent improvement.³ Both of these formulations are premises for pessimism about the future. For Aristotle, as for Plato, one resolution of this problem was in the prevention of change. Both of these philosophers created a model of society which ". . . was a static society, in which change through growth, once having conferred maturity, was thereupon to be strictly controlled to prevent innovation and the onset of decay."⁴ Obviously, the prevention of change, and fear of it, are incompatible with the idea of progress. In this regard, Bury remarked that "This prejudice against change excluded the apprehension of civilization as a progressive movement."⁵ He further suggested that the Greek's view of the world was in fact the antithesis of progressive change. Their formulations were philosophies of resignation and pessimism.⁶

Another of the classical forerunners of the idea of progress as a modern conception of history was the idea of Providence.⁷ Augustine, in *The City of God*, presented the early Christian conception of history which denied the classical Greek formulations of cycles and degeneration. To Augustine, the history of man, which was also the history of the action of Divine Providence in relation to man, ". . . traversed a fixed course, from a fixed beginning to a fixed destiny."⁸ The telic nature of man's very existence, and therefore of his history, ultimately resided in the happy destination of salvation. Several scholars are in essential agreement with the assertion that the early Christian, and particularly the Augustinian view of history, contained within it

---

³ *Ibid.*, pp. 7-20; see also George H. Hildebrand, *The Idea of Progress: A Collection of Readings*, Berkeley and Los Angeles: University of California Press, 1949, pp. 5-8. (Revised edition of a book previously edited by Frederick J. Teggart, 1929). Kenneth E. Bock, *The Acceptance of Histories*, Berkeley and Los Angeles: University of California Press, 1956, pp. 44-53; John Baillie, *The Belief in Progress*, New York: Charles Scribner's Sons, 1951, p. 6-19; Frederick J. Teggart, *Theory and Processes of History*, Berkeley and Los Angeles: University of California Press, 1941, p. 86.

⁴ Hildebrand, *op. cit.*, p. 8.

⁵ Bury, *op. cit.*, p. 11.

⁶ *Ibid.*, p. 19. In each of these historical periods we assume that the beliefs mentioned characterize the cultural elite and not necessarily the population at large.

⁷ Hildebrand, *op. cit.*, p. 4.

⁸ *Ibid.*, p. 9; Bock, *op. cit.*, pp. 57-59; Bury, *op. cit.*, p. 22; and Teggart, *op. cit.*, p. 87. See also E. Stanislaus Duzy, *Philosophy of Social Change According to the Principles of St. Thomas*, Washington, D.C.: The Catholic University of America Press, 1944, pp. 25-26.

the germs of the idea of progress.[9] Though it is true that Augustine significantly affirmed the uniqueness of historical events, the principle of order and continuity in change, and the importance of historical causation, all of which underlie the idea of progress, it is also true that he viewed the end-state as supernatural rather than temporal. Human betterment in its nonspiritual aspects was viewed as incidental to spiritual progress and to the fulfillment of The City of God.[10] Bury argues that the fundamental assumptions underlying the belief in Providence and the belief in progress are incompatible, and that the idea of progress did not gain acceptance so long as the belief in Providence was dominant.[11] Or, as Morris Ginsberg states, "The idea of progress was hardly likely to obtain wide credence until attention was shifted from the kingdom to come to the kingdom of this world. . . ."[12]

The Christian belief in the hand of Providence on the course of history began to wane in importance as it came into conflict with the rationalism of the early modern period. Particularly as the Cartesian axioms of the supremacy of reason and the invariability of the laws of nature gained acceptance, the belief in progress displaced the belief in Providence as the cause in the process of history. The fading belief in the imminence of the world's end, the new linear conception of history, and the emphasis of the universality of natural law prepared the way for the modern idea of progress.[13]

While it is certainly beyond the scope of this study to trace the gradual emergence of the idea of progress in images of the future, the basic features of the changing social and intellectual milieu should be outlined.

The first of four major features which provided the requisite conditions for the emergence of the age of progress was the scientific revolution of the seventeenth century. The developments which were occurring in the natural sciences promoted the belief in stable laws

---

[9] Duzy, *op. cit.*, p. 26; Baillie, *op. cit.*, pp. 94–98; Ernest Lee Tuveson, *Millenium and Utopia*, Berkeley and Los Angeles: University of California Press, 1949, p. 6; and John T. Marcus, "Time and the Sense of History: West and East," *Contemporary Studies in Society and History*, 3 (January, 1961), pp. 124–126.

[10] Duzy, *op. cit.*, p. 26; Bock, *op. cit.*, p. 57; and Tuveson, *op. cit.*, p. 7 .

[11] Bury, *op. cit.*, pp. 21–22.

[12] Morris Ginsberg, *The Idea of Progress: A Revaluation*, Boston: Beacon Press, 1953, p. 7. Ginsberg also notes the tendency for contemporary theologians to point to the Judao-Christian conception of history as containing the roots of the modern idea of progress. He states that, "Christian theologians seem to have become deeply interested in the idea of progress only after it became a dominant element in Western thought. The Catholic Church has on occasion explicitly repudiated it; and Protestant writers find great difficulty in coming to terms with it." See pp. 8–9.

[13] Bury, *op. cit.*, pp. 64–65; and Tuveson, *op. cit.*, pp. viii–ix, and p. 7.

of science. The spread of popular knowledge regarding the achievements of science were most important in the acceptance of the idea of progress.[14] This was not limited to natural science but was to be seen in the new scientific perspective in the study of history as well. As Mazlish has noted, "before modern man could look forward, he had to look backward in a modern way." This led to a new time perspective toward history which "eventuated in a reversed criterion as to which was 'older,' the ancient or the modern period." The consequence of this development was the rejection of the past as a major source of authority, a preliminary requirement for the growth of positive images of the future.[15]

The second development of great importance to the emergence of the doctrine of progress was the accumulation of knowledge and technology in the new sciences which culminated in the Industrial Revolution. Man's knowledge was becoming a power capable of controlling and transforming his environment. Heilbroner argues that "inventions such as the power loom and the steam engine could no longer be said merely to decorate the surface of life. . . . Nature, which had hitherto been the master of man, now became his great slave."[16] The growth of industrialism provided the basis for a new and increasingly abundant society, and further foundation for the emerging belief in progress.

The spread of popular political aspirations was the third change which promoted the idea of progress. The notions of democratic equality which gave rise to the French and American revolutions stemmed in part from the increasingly pervasive concern with the possibilities of man's control of his history. This may be seen in Condorcet's belief that the development of scientific knowledge would allow the reconciliation of "the interests of each with the interests of all."[17] Clearly, this realization of destiny as decision rather than fate promoted the popular ideology of progress. This effect of the revolution was not confined to France and the North American continent, but spread to England and elsewhere throughout Europe. Helleiner reports that ". . . even outside of France the conviction was that, with the overthrow of despotism, humanity had made the greatest stride toward its goal of perfection."[18]

---

[14] *Ibid.*, pp. 112–113; Robert L. Heilbroner, *The Future as History*, New York: Grove Press, Inc., 1961, p. 23; Mazlish, *op. cit.*, p. 448.
[15] Mazlish, *op. cit.*, pp. 448–449.
[16] Heilbroner, *op. cit.*, p. 24.
[17] Mazlish, *op. cit.*, p. 450.
[18] K. F. Helleiner, "An Essay on the Rise of Historical Pessimism in the Nineteenth Century," *Canadian Journal of Economics and Political Science*, VIII (November, 1942), p. 522.

The final feature of the changing society which provided the fundamental conditions for the rise of the idea of progress was the development of capitalism. Heilbroner suggests that the achievement of the new and desirable future turned on the presence of a framework of social and economic institutions which would allow the new technology and the new aspirations to be ". . . brought into complementary harness." The capitalist system of competition for ideas and markets ". . . literally galvanized the pace of technological and economic progress."[19] He further points to the progressive new science of economics which ". . . did indeed treat of the internal motions of society in a manner which made the future a matter of determinable calculation."[20] In Adam Smith's *Wealth of Nations*, economic progress was determined destiny even for the poor. "Progress was thus no longer a matter of hopefulness. It was a matter of predictable evolution."[21]

This very brief outline of European intellectual history since the seventeenth century could only be oversimplified in its purposive selection of those trends of change which gave rise to the idea of progress. These changes led man to believe ". . . that reform might proceed from his own aspirations, that despair could give way to determination."[22] The forces which produced such belief were to be found in the power of expanding scientific knowledge, the technology of industrialism, aspirations to political control, and the economic development of capitalism. "For the first time men began to speculate about the future in terms of a rising level of *mass* well-being, intelligence, and ideals."[23]

As pervasive as these revolutions were, their influence was restricted primarily to the people of Europe and North America. They had little large-scale effect in Asia, Africa, and Latin America. It is in these territories and among these people that we now witness the spread of these scientific, technological, political, and economic revolutions. The extension of forces which dominated the development of the Western world has, in recent years, begun to make its impact on the less developed areas. The belief in progress, the expectation of increased control of history, the idea of a meaningful future — these ideas are making their way through the developing continents and rapidly leading these people through three hundred years of history

---

[19] Heilbroner, *op. cit.*, pp. 25–26.
[20] *Ibid.*, p. 32.
[21] *Ibid.*, p. 33.
[22] *Ibid.*, p. 21.
[23] *Ibid.*, p. 27, italics in the original.

which had largely bypassed them. Their images of the future have become the focus of anxiety in the Western world. Their expectations have become instruments and objects of the cold war of ideology. As one commentator has remarked, "All thinking people today, whether they are of the Right or the Left, are concerned with the problem of the underdeveloped countries whose hungry people, the world over, no longer accept their lot as a decree of fate."[24]

The favorable image of the future in many developing countries seems to be firmly entrenched, as may be seen in findings reported by Hadley Cantril and his associates for some thirteen countries including Brazil, Cuba, Panama, Nigeria, India, Israel, the Philippines and the Dominican Republic.[25] Their findings indicate that most of the people in all of these countries held images of the future of their nation which were characterized by the pervasive optimism of high aspirations. It was also the case, with few exceptions, that most people viewed their country's present situation as better than it had been in the recent past.[26] These findings are relevant to Heilbroner's thesis concerning the schizophrenic attitude toward past and future history displayed by many underdeveloped countries. He describes this attitude as one of bitter memories of the past, combined with a reaching for the future with enthusiasm. He states, "Hopefully, and under good leadership, the latter attitude will come to predominate."[27] Cantril's findings would seem to fulfill Heilbroner's hopes at least partially. For example, in Cuba in the spring of 1960, more than a year after Castro came to power, Cubans of all economic levels viewed their country's future and recent past as progressive. Brazilians in the spring of 1961 were similarly confident about the future progress of their nation.

The idea of progress is thus no longer the preserve of the Western world. Indeed, it seems that even as many intellectual and scholarly circles in Europe and America repudiated belief in progress,[28] their colonials and otherwise subject peoples had begun to concern them-

[24] Leo Huberman, "A Suggestion to HUAC," *Monthly Review*, XV (June, 1963), p. 89.
[25] Hadley Cantril, *The Pattern of Human Concerns*, New Brunswick, N. J.: Rutgers University Press, 1965; Hadley Cantril and Lloyd A. Free, "Hopes and Fears for Self and Country," *The American Behavioral Scientist* (supplement), VI (October, 1962), pp. 2–30; Hadley Cantril, "A Study of Aspirations," *Scientific American*, 208 (February, 1963), pp. 41–55; see also Sybil H. May, "The Tonic of Revolution," *Monthly Review*, XV (June, 1963), pp. 80–86.
[26] Cantril, *The Pattern of Human Concerns, op. cit.*, especially Part III.
[27] Heilbroner, *op. cit.*, p. 80.
[28] See Crane Brinton's lucid discussion of this problem in "Utopia and Democracy," in *Daedalus*, 94 (Spring, 1965), pp. 348–366. He laments that the belief in progress, ". . . though not dead, [is] very much weakened among the intellectual few."

selves with the possibilities of progress. The extension of popular political participation in the developing countries and the dismantlement of colonial empires have provided the political revolution which has historically promoted concern with future progress. Technological and economic development promoted by the advanced protagonists of progress are partially inducing the economic revolution. The necessary social and economic institutions are being created. History is no longer the product of fate alone for the underdeveloped areas. The possibility of progress is being incorporated into their images of the future.

SOCIAL CHANGE AND IMAGES OF THE FUTURE

In Jamaica, as in many other developing countries, numerous aspects of social change have become the objects of history-making decisions. It has been argued that in the advanced nations of the Western world, economic and political development are less manipulable, and are not features of change which are consciously amenable to history-making.[29] In the developing countries today, this need not be the case; and in Jamaica it does not seem to be the case. Wendell Bell has written with reference to Jamaica:

> Conscious direction of the polity, economy, and society became the preoccupation of the new indigenous elite. What should be done? How should it be done? What should Jamaica's national goals be? How can they be best achieved? . . . the transfer of power from a colonial to an indigenous regime forcefully raises a large number of societal policies which become highly problematic, subject to change, and, most of all, potentially amenable to manipulation in accordance with the collective will of the citizens and the leaders of the new nation.[30]

Within this context of directed change, Bell reports findings which bear on Jamaica's decisions regarding the form of the political system, the nature of the social structure, the selection of global alignments, and the nature of Jamaica's social and cultural history.

In these societies in which features such as these are amenable to history-making by conscious decision, the images of the future held by the leadership, their attitudes toward change, and specifically their ex-

---

[29] For example, see Heilbroner's discussion, "The Limits of the Possible," *op. cit.*, pp. 181–184.

[30] Wendell Bell, *Jamaican Leaders: Political Attitudes in a New Nation*, Berkeley and Los Angeles: University of California Press, 1964, pp. 87–88, a more detailed discussion of such decisions may be found in Wendell Bell and Ivar Oxaal, *Decisions of Nationhood: Political and Social Development in the British Caribbean*, Denver, Colo.: Social Science Foundation, University of Denver Press, 1964.

pectations regarding the nation's potential are critically important. Insofar as present decisions are future-oriented they are based not only on knowledge and values, but on expectations concerning a future state of affairs. "In other words, a decision is an act, or a series of acts, involving the simultaneous manipulation of facts, values, and above all, expectations."[31] Decision-making "turns in part upon a picture of significant changes in the emerging future."[32] Therein lies the importance of images of the future.

Numerous theorists have asserted the creative power of future expectations in the realization of the future. For lack of empirical data, I shall call upon some of these to support my contention that belief in progress as an image of the future is important in shaping that future.

The negative case seems least difficult. Resistance to change which may reside in the pessimistic or nihilistic view of human nature is most obvious. Gunnar Myrdal has contended that "the pessimistic view of human nature is, and has always been, the deepest sense of a conservative argument."[33] Similarly, R. N. Sanford and associates have concluded that "the pessimist, belittling the likelihood of appreciable or significant progress, by his attitude adds obstacles to practical accomplishment and facilitates the very failure which he anticipates."[34] Thus, these authors contend that pessimism may indeed be a strong brake on effective action, and a source for the *status quo*.

It has also been suggested that pessimism or cynicism might be a more realistic outlook in some situations. Irving Louis Horowitz has written, "Ours is an age of pessimism. Camus, in fact, once declared that the only properly twentieth-century posture is cynicism."[35] Recalling the horrors of Hitlerism and Hiroshima, and the ever-present threat of nuclear warfare, he suggests that Camus' sentiment cannot be easily dismissed. Although dissatisfaction with the present and the history from which it emerged may be quite reasonable, it is also true that the projection of these views into the future can be a self-fulfilling prophecy

---

[31] Heinz Eulau, "H. D. Lasswell's Developmental Analysis," *The Western Political Quarterly*, XI (June, 1958), p. 230.

[32] Harold D. Lasswell, "Legal Education and Public Policy," in the *Analysis of Political Behavior*, New York: Oxford University Press, 1948, p. 30, as quoted in Eulau, *ibid*.

[33] Gunnar Myrdal, *Population: A Problem for Democracy*, London: Oxford University Press, 1940, p. 13, as quoted in K. F. Helleiner, *op. cit.*, p. 514.

[34] R. Nevitt Sanford, Herbert S. Conrad, and Kate Franck, "Psychological Determinants of Optimism Regarding Consequences of War," *The Journal of Psychology*, XXVI (1946), p. 235.

[35] Irving Louis Horowitz, "Another View From Our Left," *New Politics*, II (Winter, 1963), p. 77.

that engenders a style of behavior that ensures the dire outcome.[36] In this regard Wilbert E. Moore has remarked:

> Though the historic death rate of nations, and especially political regimes, has been rather high, for a nation's leaders to admit to possible failure of indefinite national survival would only assure an early demise. The belief in an endless future is a necessary, though not sufficient, condition for any future at all.[37]

As an image of the future, cynicism and pessimism are anticipations of impotence, and tacit acceptance of future history as fate rather than decision. Concluding his discussion of the self-fulfilling prophecy, Robert K. Merton wrote, "It is only with the rejection of social fatalism . . . that the tragic circle of fear, social disaster, and reinforced fear can be broken."[38] The impotent character of pessimism can only support that social fatalism. Karl Marx declared that such "Impotence expresses itself in a single proposition — the maintenance of the *status quo*."[39]

UNESCO has postulated that "wars begin in the minds of men."[40] Analyzing the role of expectancy in international tension, Gordon W. Allport has used this postulate as a point of departure. He states, "The crux of the matter lies in the fact that while most people deplore war, they nonetheless *expect* it to continue. And what people expect determines their behavior."[41] In a similar discussion of the role of expectancy, Raymond Aron correctly points to the probability that the expectation of war was induced by real and not imaginary facts, and he cautions against confusing facts and expectations as cause and effect.[42] While the relevance of this warning should be clear, it remains that expectations, whether based on fact or fantasy, do influence decisions which shape the future.

In his recent two volume work, *The Image of the Future*, F. L. Polak asserts that the history of mankind can be written as the history of its images of the future. He takes as his major thesis the idea that man's

---

[36] Robert K. Merton, "The Self-Fulfilling Prophecy," in *Social Theory and Social Structure* (rev. ed.), Glencoe, Ill.: The Free Press, 1957, pp. 421–436.
[37] Wilbert E. Moore, *Man, Time, and Society*, New York: John Wiley and Sons, Inc., 1963, p. 152.
[38] Merton, *op. cit.*, p. 436.
[39] Horowitz, *op. cit.*, p. 88.
[40] William Buchanan and Hadley Cantril, *How Nations See Each Other*, Urbana: University of Illinois Press, 1953, p. 11.
[41] Gordon W. Allport, "The Role of Expectancy," in Hadley Cantril (ed.), *Tensions That Cause Wars*, Urbana: University of Illinois Press, 1950, p. 43, italics in the original.
[42] Raymond Aron, "Conflict and War from the Viewpoint of Historical Sociology," in *The Nature of Conflict*, Paris: UNESCO, 1957, p. 188.

images of the future by his purposeful intervention shape the actual future.⁴³ Polak's discussion of the interaction between images of the future and eventual future outcomes is quite consistent with Lasswell's earlier statements regarding the future-oriented character of decision-making processes. In Eulau's summary of Lasswell's developmental analysis we find the statement that ". . . 'among the factors moulding the future are interpretations of the future.' And . . . expectations of the future have an impact on action, notably policy decisions. . . ."⁴⁴

Wilbert E. Moore has recently tried to convince sociologists of the utility of creative thinking about future states of human affairs that would more closely approximate individual and collective goals. He states that "The utility of utopias is simple. In the degree that utopias are taken seriously, they determine the course of present action and become, in a restricted sense, self-fulfilling."⁴⁵

Images of the future have also been central in the work of Jiri Nehnevajsa concerning the cold war, ideological conflict, and decision-making. He suggests that not only do anticipated futures provide clues to present behavior, but furthermore, "As the anticipations of the future forecast the present decisions and behavior, the future itself is in the making."⁴⁶

Bell and Oxaal, in their discussion of societal values and their importance for men's aspirations and decisions of social policy, have similarly underscored the creative power of man's images of the future. They point to ". . . an obvious, but often forgotten truth; to an increasing degree men are masters of their collective destiny. . . . What men do depends in part on their beliefs about the present and in part on their images of the future, especially on their values concerning the good society."⁴⁷

Each of these theorists has asserted, in varying contexts and from different points of view, that expectations about the future have an

⁴³ F. L. Polak, *The Image of the Future*, 2 vols., New York: Oceana Publications, 1961.

⁴⁴ Eulau, *op. cit.*, p. 237.

⁴⁵ See Moore's Presidential Address delivered at the annual meeting of the American Sociological Association in Miami Beach, Florida, August 31, 1966. *American Sociological Review*, 31 (December, 1966), pp. 765–772.

⁴⁶ Jiri Nehnevajsa, "Outcomes Approach to Personal Decision-Making," University of Pittsburgh, October, 1963, (mimeographed). See also his "Applications of Cold War Outcomes," prepared for the meetings of the American Association for Public Opinion Research, Lake George, New York, May 18-20, 1962; "Elements of Project Theory: From Concept to Design," Air Force Office of Scientific Research, Technical Note TN-60-6 October, 1960, (mimeographed); and "Anticipatory Analysis of Ideological Conflict," presented at the meetings of the American Sociological Association, New York, N. Y., 1960.

⁴⁷ Bell and Oxaal, *op. cit.*, p. 85.

influence on the realization of that future. In deference to Professor W. I. Thomas, his more general statement of the reality of one's definition of a situation should also be acknowledged. A statement made by Charles A. Beard in the Introduction to *The Idea of Progress* by J. B. Bury, seems a fitting summary. He wrote: "So it may be ventured that if the idea of progress is not a stubborn outcome of true history, it may, as a faith in possibilities, actually make history."[48]

AN OVERVIEW

I have argued that man's thoughts about his existence in time — his history, what he is, what he might have been, and what he might possibly be — are of critical importance for his choices and decisions concerning what he ought to be. Moore has suggested that such a sense of time is intrinsic to the human condition, and moreover, that almost all of man's personal and collective concerns are bounded by time.[49] These temporal orientations of human life can be interpreted as value orientations which give order and direction to the actions and thoughts which constitute social life.[50] In an extension of Oswald Spengler's thesis that cultures may be differentiated by the meanings that they give to time, Kluckhohn and Strodtbeck assert that a great deal can be predicted about the direction of change in a society if one knows the people's conceptions of past, present, and future.[51] To the extent that their proposition is acceptable, we should attach even greater significance to knowing the views of the past and images of the future held by a society's leaders. This significance is further enhanced in situations in which those leaders are overtly concerned with planning change, which necessarily involves not only a choice of goals, but also an image of the trends of the future. As de Jouvenel argues, "If our actions, which shape the future, are themselves shaped by our views of the future, these latter surely are of the utmost importance."[52] It is these views of the future held by public leaders in Jamaica that we shall be concerned with in this book.

The purpose of the research reported here is to analyze attitudes toward social, economic, and political changes that were taking place in Jamaica during the transition from colonial to politically independ-

---

[48] Bury, *op. cit.*, p. xxviii.
[49] Moore, *Man, Time, and Society, op. cit.*, pp. 7–9.
[50] Florence Rockwood Kluckhohn and Fred L. Strodtbeck, *Variations in Value Orientations*, Evanston, Ill.: Row, Peterson and Co., 1961, p. 4.
[51] *Ibid.*, p. 14; see also Florence Rockwood Kluckhohn, "Dominant and Substitute Profiles of Cultural Orientations: Their Significance for the Analysis of Social Stratification," *Social Forces*, 28 (May, 1950), p. 380.
[52] Bertrand de Jouvenel, (ed.), *Futuribles I*, Geneva: Droz, 1963, p. ix.

ent status. Specifically, variation in belief in progress is described and analyzed by reference to the social characteristics, ideological commitments, power, and knowledge of a group of Jamaican leaders. The universe of leaders studied is made up of persons who were influential in policy formulation and implementation in relation to West Kingston, the island's largest area of urban lower-class residence. These leaders include Members of Parliament, Cabinet Ministers, and some prominent solicitors and businessmen, all of whom had a reputation for playing an important role regarding the urban lower-class area and the problems of the people there.[53]

In the analysis to follow, these leaders' attitudes toward the island-nation's potential for progress are discussed in relation to their commitment to egalitarianism, their relative power in public affairs, and their knowledge of the discontents of the urban lower-class people whose future is significantly linked with the future of the nation.[54] These three variables are in turn used to analyze the leaders' views of the urban lower classes who comprise the focus of their community responsibilities. Finally, at several points, data collected among the urban lower classes are compared with the findings for the leaders in order to provide a test of the reality of some of the beliefs expressed by the leaders. This research is perhaps best viewed as an exploratory and descriptive study. The conclusions drawn and interpretations suggested are necessarily tentative, and should serve as the baseline for continuing inquiry. The study began with a focus on planned change and attitudes toward those changes, and although the findings have led somewhat away from that focus, I think the resulting reinterpretation does a better job, than did the original focus, of conveying the social realities of the Jamaican situation, and of tying this case study to the dynamics of change that exist in the developing societies throughout the world today.

[53] For a detailed description of the universe of leaders interviewed, the methodology by which that universe was defined, and a discussion of data collection, see Appendix 1.
[54] This important link between the future of the nation as a whole and that of West Kingston and the growing lower classes who live there is discussed further below.

CHAPTER 2 Jamaica: Yesterday and Today

The tri-colored flag raised over the island of Jamaica on August 6, 1962 marked the political independence of this nation of 1.7 million people. Jamaica is a high-peaked island of nearly 5,000 square miles located south of Cuba and west of the Republic of Haiti in the Caribbean Sea. It is 150 miles in length from east to west, and the greatest distance between the northern and southern coasts is 50 miles. The achievement of Dominion status within the British Commonwealth of nations was the most recent in a long line of social and constitutional changes which will eventually lead to Jamaica's development as an integrated and self-determining society. Whether it is dated from the riots on the sugar estates at Frome and the wharves of Kingston in 1938, from the Morant Bay Rebellion of 1865, or from the abolition of slavery in 1838, this trend of change is affecting the lives of more and more Jamaicans as the drive for progress has gained momentum. The heritage of slavery and the ills of colonial exploitation have been no small challenge to the people of Jamaica; they have also given strength and experience in overcoming injustices.

FROM COLUMBUS TO BUSTAMANTE

In May, 1494, Columbus landed on the northern coast of Jamaica and found the island inhabited solely by Arawak Indians.[1] Spanish colonization followed with the establishment of New Seville in 1509.

[1] This summary is drawn from F. R. Augier, S. C. Gordon, D. G. Hall, and M. Reckord, *The Making of the West Indies*, London: Longmans, 1960; Phillip D. Curtin, *Two Jamaicas*, Cambridge: Harvard University Press, 1955; W. F. Gardner, *A History of Jamaica*, London: T. Fisher Unwin, 2nd edition, 1909; Douglas Hall, *Free Jamaica, 1838–1865*, New Haven: Yale University Press, 1959; J. H. Parry and P. M. Sherlock, *A Short History of the West Indies*, London: MacMillan and Co., 1956; *Development Towards Self-Government in the Caribbean*, a symposium held under the auspices of the Netherlands Universities Foundation for International Cooperation at The Hague, September, 1954. The Hague: W. van Hoeve, Ltd., 1955; Morley Ayearst, *The British West Indies: The Search for Self-Government*, New York: New York University Press, 1960.

After brief and largely unsuccessful attempts at gold mining, for which the enslaved Arawaks provided the labor, the Spanish turned their new possession to agricultural and pastoral uses to supply their continuing expeditions in the New World. During this period of Spanish dominance, the Indian population of the island was virtually exterminated despite some vigorous though belated attempts to protect them. A second event of lasting significance was the introduction of the first African slaves to the island.

A British expedition took Jamaica from the Spanish in May, 1655. Having been humiliated in battle with the Spanish forces at Hispaniola, British naval forces landed in Jamaica and drove the Spanish from their capital at St. Jago de la Vega. After a few years of sporadic fighting between the British and some Spanish guerillas and their slaves, the Spaniards acquiesced and left the island. The years of British rule that followed saw the establishment of a plantation economy based on sugar and slavery, and the development of a society dominated by an oligarchy of white planters and merchants. During this period it is estimated that some 700,000 African slaves were imported to Jamaica to labor in the fields and houses of the plantocracy. Until the nineteeth century Jamaica prospered as one of the largest producers of sugar and remained one of Britain's most highly valued colonial possessions. The eclipse of sugar and the resulting decline of Jamaica's importance to the imperial power began with the abolition of the slave trade in 1807, and was further ensured by the Emancipation Act and England's move toward free trade, including the gradual removal of colonial preferential duties.

Some major consequences of emancipation were to be seen in Jamaican political developments in the next few decades. The stability of the Old Representative System of a Governor and Council appointed by the Crown, and an elected Assembly, had been weakened by continuing battles between the Crown and the Assembly with the Governor most often caught in the middle. Throughout the British West Indies, the white dominated Assemblies were subjected to continued pressure from Britain to allow greater participation by the expanding white and colored middle classes. The Jamaican Assembly, the elected legislature of the old system, became less and less representative and more and more irresponsible, and refused to take action to improve the worsening conditions of the masses of new citizens. The Morant Bay "Rebellion" of 1865, and the violently repressive reaction that followed were instrumental in the retrogression to Crown Colony government which was to last for almost eighty years. Thus by mid-1886, the Jamaican Assembly had abolished elections and representative government, and, with the exception of the addition in 1884 and 1895, of some members of the legislature who were elected by restricted franchise, Jamaica was ruled by the Crown until 1944.

Sugar continued the struggle through this difficult period, its fortunes fluctuating with the world sugar market. In the face of the developing beet sugar industry in Europe and increased competition from other cane producers, the agricultural economy of Jamaica was ripe for the introduction of bananas in 1870 as a supplementary export crop. Indeed, by 1912, the "green gold" of bananas alone made up more than half the value of Jamaica's exports, and continued as a major crop until the 1930's when the plants were decimated by disease. It was also in the early 1930's that sugar began its timely revival with the advent of Tate and Lyle and the West Indies Sugar Company, and the re-establishment of industry supports in the form of imperial preferences and guaranteed markets. Sugar's new peak of prosperity did not come until World War II when the demand for West Indian sugar greatly increased.

In 1936, the inertia which had been Jamaica for nearly eighty years began to stir with men of ideas and thoughts of mass participation born out of the need for self-government. The beginnings of a labor movement appeared; popular leadership emerged; a political party was formed. The masses became a decisive power behind the constitutional reforms which culminated in Jamaica's independence in August, 1962.[2]

The rise of local nationalist interest among a small cadre of the colored middle class marked the beginnings of a new era of politics. The appearance of the National Reform Association founded by Ken Hill in 1937, the formation in New York City of the Jamaica Progressive League, and the publication by H. P. Jacobs of *Public Opinion*, a nationalist news weekly, all represented a growing group of critics and social reformers. From them came thoughts of self-government, adult suffrage, the growing proletariat, the relevance of socialism, and the organization of labor, all against the background of an increasingly discontented population facing declining wages and increasing unemployment.

A series of strikes began in 1937, first among banana laborers, followed in January, 1938, by a strike of the sugar workers at the Serge

---

[2] This discussion is based on the following sources: C. Paul Bradley, "Mass Parties in Jamaica: Structure and Organization," *Social and Economic Studies*, IX (December, 1960), pp. 375–416; H. P. Jacobs, "The Self-Government Movement," *The Daily Gleaner*, Kingston, May 10, 1955, reprinted in *Independence Anthology of Jamaican Literature*, Kingston: United Printers, 1962, pp. 205–214; O. W. Phelps, "Rise of the Labour Movement in Jamaica," *Social and Economic Studies*, IX (December, 1960), pp. 417–468; and *The Handbook of Jamaica for 1961*, Kingston: The Government Printer, 1962, p. 43.

Island estate in the parish of St. Thomas. The militant spirit seemed contagious as another strike of major proportions occurred at the West Indies Sugar Company's Frome estate in April, 1938. On the heels of the Frome affair came the first of many demonstrations in metropolitan Kingston, which lasted from May 9, until the climax on the morning of May 23, 1938. What began with relatively orderly demonstrations by unemployed workers and meetings of striking dock workers, became general disorder and rioting. By the evening of May 23, a force of approximately 1,000 men, including police, constables, and several platoons of troops, was patrolling the city in an effort to quell looting, burning, and generally to restore order. By the end of the month, Kingston was quiet, but the disturbances which had again spread to the countryside continued until early June, 1938.

Jamaica's mass-based labor and political organizations, and the first significant popular leaders emerged from this turbulent period. Sir William Alexander Bustamante, whose prominence and popularity resulted from his flamboyant leadership and timely agitation during the disturbances, founded the Bustamante Industrial Trade Union (BITU). In some respects, the fiery Bustamante's career was bolstered by the Governor, A. F. Richards, who ordered his internment in 1940, for seventeen months because of an inflammatory speech he made in Kingston. It was during his internment that Busta's cousin, Norman Washington Manley, Rhodes Scholar and Oxford-educated barrister, did the primary organizing work for the BITU as a "caretaker" of the union. Manley, a member of the Trade Union Congress, and an important mediator in the many crises of that period, had recently launched the Peoples' National Party (PNP), a moderate socialist party in the Fabian tradition. One would expect that Manley saw complementary gains to be made for his party and his cousin's union, and that together they would be the popular basis for the drive to national self-determination. At this point both organizations had overlapping memberships, and Bustamante himself had been a member of the PNP since 1939. This harmony was not long lived however, as Bustamante, upon his release from detention early in 1942, split with Manley and the PNP. This separation set the stage for the political rivalry which was to dominate Jamaican politics for more than twenty years.

THE NEW ERA

The polity. The first truly representative government was established in Jamaica in 1944 with the introduction of a new constitution which provided for universal adult suffrage and a popularly elected House of Representatives. On the eve of the 1944 elections, the first under the new constitution, Bustamante founded the Jamaica Labour Party (JLP) as a political extension of the BITU. A third party, the Jamaica Democratic Party, which represented the land owners and mercantile community, also planned to contest the election. The results showed Bustamante and the Jamaica Labour Party had won 22 of the 32 seats in the House of Representatives (with 41.4 per cent of the total vote), and the People's National Party had won in five constituencies (23.5 per cent of the vote). The remaining five seats were won by independent candidates. The businessman's Jamaica Democratic Party failed to capture a single seat. Thus the JLP with Busta at its head formed the first popular government.

In 1949, the JLP repeated its victory by winning 17 seats to the PNP's 13, and two for independent candidates. Perhaps here the tide had begun to turn in favor of the PNP however, as they gained more of the total vote than the JLP. In the general election of 1955 the PNP were finally able to oust Busta and the Labour Party by winning 18 seats to the JLP's 14 seats. By this time the PNP had shed much of the trappings of its earlier socialist program, and had in 1952 purged the party of four members who were alleged to be communists. This led to the disaffiliation of the Trade Union Congress from the PNP, which in turn prompted the PNP to organize a labor wing in the form of the National Worker's Union (NWU) in 1952. Both the removal of some of the alleged "red fringe" of the party, and the organization of the NWU may have helped the PNP to victory in 1955.

Additional constitutional changes in 1949, 1953, 1956, 1957, and 1959 established a ministerial system and provided more and more local autonomy of government. Again in 1959, the PNP won the general elections, this time with an increased majority in the House of Representatives, and nearly 55 per cent of the island vote. Meanwhile, in 1958, Jamaica had united with the other British Caribbean territories in the short-lived West Indies Federation. The federal wing of the JLP, the Democratic Labour Party, swept the federal elections in Jamaica, winning 11 of 17 seats in the federal parliament.

A swell of anti-federation sentiment led by Bustamante and the JLP resulted in Premier Manley's calling a referendum to decide whether Jamaica would remain in the federal association. In September, 1961, after a highly partisan campaign, the people of Jamaica voted to withdraw from the Federation. Manley immediately began negotiations for the independence of Jamaica and called general elections for April 10, 1962, to allow the people to choose the leadership of the new nation.

These elections of 1962 were contested by the two major parties as well as a new third party, The People's Political Party, formed in 1961 by Millard Johnson. Assuming the clear importance of racial appeals

Jamaica's Capital City, Kingston. (*Courtesy of Jamaica Tourist Board*).

Kingston Industrial Estate. (*Courtesy of Jamaica Industrial Development Commission*).

Worker in the cane. *(Courtesy of Sugar Manufacturers' Association).*

Transporting cane to the mill. *(Courtesy of Sugar Manufacturers' Association).*

Bauxite loading facilities at Kaiser Port. (*Courtesy of Jamaica Industrial Development Commission*).

Alcan Jamaica Limited's alumina plant at Ewarton. (*Courtesy of Jamaica Industrial Development Commission*).

Gordon House, the meeting place of the national legislature. *(Courtesy of Jamaica Information Service).*

The interior of Gordon House. *(Courtesy of Government Public Relations Office).*

Jamaica House, the official residence of the Prime Minister. (*Courtesy of Jamaica Information Service*).

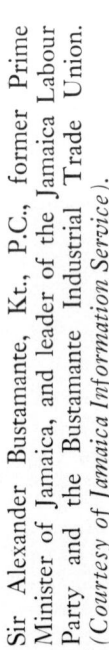

Sir Alexander Bustamante, Kt., P.C., former Prime Minister of Jamaica, and leader of the Jamaica Labour Party and the Bustamante Industrial Trade Union. (*Courtesy of Jamaica Information Service*).

Sir Clifford Campbell, G.C.M.G., G.C.V.O., Governor-General of Jamaica. (*Courtesy of Jamaica Information Service*).

to the depressed segments of Jamaicans, the new party under Johnson's leadership, recalled the name of Marcus Garvey and donned the symbols of African nationalism, preaching freedom and equality for black people. Although African tribal robes were an innovation in Jamaican politics, the ideological and practical appeals had long ago been sounded by the major parties. The campaign and the election results were little affected by the new party which failed to obtain even 1 per cent of the vote. Bustamante and the JLP were successful in the election, gaining 26 seats to the PNP's 19.[3] The PNP aligned themselves as pro-federationists in the 1961 referendum, and lost that battle only to face the electorate again in a few months, this time at a decided disadvantage. The successful JLP campaign was based largely on attacks on Manley, "The Man With The Plan," the man who had wanted to keep Jamaica in the weakening Federation, and the man whose high-flown schemes for national development had largely benefitted the middle and upper classes while the mass of Jamaicans still waited for improvements. The PNP's decision to base their campaign largely on Manley, the man and leader, rather than on the party, the relatively successful government, and PNP accomplishments, clearly provided the target for the JLP campaign. From that contest Sir William Alexander Bustamante emerged as victor, and this time also as the first Prime Minister of independent Jamaica.

Since 1962 when the data for this study were collected there have been several major occurrences in Jamaican politics, including the first serious confrontation with the problems of leadership succession, the incorporation of new younger leaders in the hierarchies of both parties, and the first general elections since independence. The charismatic Bustamante, now in his 80's, was incapacitated by illness for varying periods during his term as Prime Minister and had to retire from active politics. Although Busta formally retained his post as Prime Minister and leader of the JLP, Mr. Donald B. Sangster, Minister of Finance since 1962, and Deputy Labour Party Leader since 1950, became Deputy Prime Minister and later Acting Prime Minister. He also took over Busta's portfolios of Defense and External Affairs.

Busta's age and illness and the impending general elections set the stage for one of the rare power struggles among the top leadership of the Labour Party. What had been covert maneuvering broke into the open because the person holding the position of First Deputy Leader of the Party would be the JLP standard bearer in the election campaign, and would almost certainly be the Prime Minister if the party were to win. Busta's apparently chosen successor, Senator Hugh L.

---

[3] *Report of the Chief Electoral Officer, General Elections, 1962,* Kingston: The Government Printer, 1962, p. 4.

Shearer, Minister without portfolio and Island Supervisor of the BITU, supported Sangster against the challenger, Robert Lightbourne, the Minister of Trade and Industry. This gave Sangster a decisive victory in the annual party convention, and after patching many of the breaches in the party ranks he went on to lead the Labourites in the 1967 election campaign.

Meanwhile, since its defeat in the 1962 elections, the PNP had been struggling through an agonizing reappraisal of its organization and policies. It was decided that the National Worker's Union should have greater strength in the party, and from the turmoil of annual conferences and meetings of the National Executive of the party there emerged a new but familiar looking policy statement that indicated the disenchantment of many PNP leaders with the middle-of-the-road position of the last ten years. It also showed the mettle of the more radical minds among the party hierarchy. The new PNP program, reminiscent of their *Plan for Today* of 1940, called for a return to democratic socialism, nationalization of selected public utilities, a large measure of land reform and redistribution of inefficiently used land, a new revenue and financial policy, and an independent neutralist stance in foreign affairs. Despite the party's acceptance of this program, the equivocation and uncertainty regarding the firmness of its socialist commitment could be seen in the retention of the moderates in the controlling posts of the party executive, and in the expulsion of the none too reverent leaders of the Young Socialist League for reasons of "subversive activities" against the party and union. To the radicals in the PNP, the rest of the leadership lacked the hardheaded determination necessary to adhere to a socialist program, and particularly among the young, Manley's charisma was waning. The PNP went into the elections somewhat divided by this internal disagreement on policy.

As the elections drew closer, the government electoral office and a Parliamentary committee on constituency boundaries were preparing the battleground. New voters lists were compiled on the basis of a new system of enumeration and registration involving fingerprinting of voters throughout the island as well as photographs of voters in prescribed urban constituencies of Kingston and St. Andrew. Working from these new lists, Parliament drew new constituency boundaries and increased the number of seats from 45 to 53.

After a short campaign marked by sporadic incidents of violence in the urban areas, the Jamaican electorate went to the polls on February 21, 1967, and again returned the Jamaica Labour Party to power. The fact that the Labour-dominated constituency boundaries committee had done its job well could be seen in the distribution of seats and votes. The JLP won 33 and the PNP 20 of the total of 53 seats, yet less than 5,000 votes (about 1 per cent) separated the parties in total popular vote. The PNP decried the election as a "bogus election" and a "rape of democracy," because of the alleged disenfranchisement of some 300,000 voters under the new registration system. Although it is clear that a large percentage of the electorate were denied their opportunity to vote by the inefficiencies of the registration procedures, it is less obvious what the effect of more complete voters list might have been on the outcome of the election.

Mr. Donald B. Sangster had successfully led the Labour Party campaign, and was immediately sworn in as Jamaica's new Prime Minister, only to have the honor he deserved and the position he had won taken from him by illness and death within a few weeks of his victory. Sangster's tragic and untimely death reopened the battle of leadership succession in the party, but this time the heir-apparent seemed more obvious. After some painful deliberations and maneuvering, the JLP parliamentary group named Hugh L. Shearer, trade union leader and Minister of External Affairs, to be the new Prime Minister.

Broadly speaking, the elections in Jamaica have developed a fairly regular pattern of support for the parties. Both of the major parties have had continued support from some segments of the commercial community, and the JLP has commanded greater support from the large landowners. The JLP has also been favored by the rural agricultural working classes, while the PNP has drawn the support of the urban middle classes and skilled laborers. The urban lower classes have remained largely unpredictable and have tended to alternate in their support of candidates from the major parties, though the JLP made some surprising gains here in 1967.

The Economy. The Jamaica Labour Party took control of the government in 1962, after seven years in opposition. During those years Jamaica had experienced considerable economic growth. The foundations laid by the JLP in their earlier tenure as government and the program of industrialization pursued by the PNP had begun to pay off. References to the commonly used indices of economic growth would depict Jamaica as a nation which has found the key to dynamic progress toward economic self-maintenance. The exploitation of bauxite, the expansion of the tourist industry, and increases in small manufacturing brought phenomenal growth in the last decade.

For example, as shown in Table 1, the Gross National Product in current values increased from £114.6 million in 1953 to £260 million in 1962.[4] Similarly, the increases in gross fixed capital investment have

[4] *Five Year Independence Plan, 1963–1968*, Kingston: The Government Printer, 1963, p. 12; see also *Economic Survey, Jamaica, 1961.* The Central Planning Unit, Government of Jamaica, 1962, p. 28.

Social Change and Images of The Future

Table 1. ANNUAL INCREASES IN GROSS NATIONAL PRODUCT: 1953–1962*

Year	Gross National Product**	Annual Increase	Annual Increase (Per Cent)
1953	114.6	—	—
1954	127.7	13.1	11.4
1955	145.3	17.6	13.8
1956	166.7	21.4	14.7
1957	199.6	32.9	19.7
1958	206.9	7.3	3.7
1959	221.8	14.9	7.2
1960	240.2	18.4	8.3
1961	254.6	14.4	6.0
1962	260.0	5.4	2.1

* *Five Year Independence Plan, 1963–1968*, Kingston: The Government Printer, 1963, p. 12.
** Current values in £ millions sterling.

been sizeable both from foreign and domestic sources. The national income figures, when adjusted for price increases, show a rate of increase of about 7 per cent per annum for the years 1953 to 1959. This is considerably higher than the rate of population growth as reflected in the per capita income figures given in Table 2.[5] Jamaica's

Table 2. NATIONAL INCOME PER CAPITA, 1955–1962*

Year	National Income In £'000	Population At Year End	Income Per Capita in £
1955	125,108	1,468,128	85.2
1956	143,233	1,494,648	95.8
1957	170,995	1,525,176	112.1
1958	177,265	1,564,747	113.3
1959	188,630	1,599,781	117.9
1960	204,909	1,624,647	126.1
1961	215,203	1,638,676	131.3
1962	225,100	1,662,079	135.4

* *Annual Abstract of Statistics, 1962*, Kingston, Jamaica: Department of Statistics, 1964, p. 40.

average annual rate of growth in Gross Domestic Product per capita was 7.8 per cent for the years 1950–1959. This figure was higher than that achieved by any of the fourteen Latin American and Caribbean

[5] *Ibid.*, and the *Annual Abstract of Statistics, 1961*, Kingston: Department of Statistics, 1962, p. 62.

countries for which these data were readily available, including Puerto Rico and oil-rich Venezuela.[6]

It should also be noted that the growth rates began a relative decline again in the late 1950's and early 1960's. In fact, the extraordinarily high rates of growth in the mid-1950's were due primarily to the discovery of bauxite, some increases in industrial development and the construction industries, and the reactions of other sectors of the economy to these unusual increases. There were marked increases in capital expenditures from the early 1950's until 1958, reflecting the new facilities for the extraction and processing of bauxite, the construction of a cement plant, and various other projects. Since the completion of many of the projects, and perhaps due to some coincidental influence of a "wait-and-see" attitude regarding the political situation surrounding Federation and independence, capital expenditure declined somewhat in its contribution to Gross National Product.

The percentage contributions of certain significant sectors to the Gross Domestic Product over the period 1938 to 1962, are shown in Table 3. Despite the fact that more than a third of Jamaica's labor

Table 3. PERCENTAGE CONTRIBUTION OF SELECTED INDUSTRIAL SECTORS TO GROSS DOMESTIC PRODUCT AT FACTOR COST, 1938–1962*

Industrial Sectors	1938	1950	1957	1961	1962
Agriculture, forestry and fishing	36.2	30.8	13.8	12.7	12.4
Mining	—	—	8.8	8.6	8.8
Manufacturing	6.5	11.3	12.7	13.3	13.3
Construction and Installation	3.5	7.6	13.6	11.2	10.8
Total Gross Domestic Product**	—	70.1	191.9	244.3	252.5

* Drawn from the Jamaican Government's *Five Year Independence Plan, 1963–1968*, Kingston: The Government Printer, 1963, p. 13.
** Total Gross Domestic Product at factor cost in current values.

force are still in the agricultural sector, there has been a marked decline in its percentage contribution to the Gross Domestic Product, and only a slight increase in its absolute contribution in recent years. These low rates of growth in agriculture are probably due in part to the great number of small cultivations. The low relative growth in agriculture has been dwarfed in recent years by the marked expansion

[6] *Statistical Abstract of Latin America, 1962*, Los Angeles: Center for Latin American Studies, University of California, Los Angeles, 1963, p. 70.

of mining, manufacturing, and construction. For example, prior to the discovery and extraction of bauxite the mining sector's contribution was negligible, but in 1953 its contribution to the Gross Domestic Product was about two per cent, and by 1957 this had increased to nearly nine per cent, and has remained at that level. Similarly, manufacturing increases have been considerable and have been accompanied by the diversification of products.[7]

These changes in the composition of the contributions to the Gross Domestic Product were reflected in the growth and changing composition of Jamaica's external trade also. A sharp increase in total domestic exports from about £17.3 million in 1952 to £62.1 million in 1962 was due mainly to the development and exporting of bauxite resources. In 1952, various food products including sugar, bananas, citrus, and pimento made up 80 per cent of domestic exports, whereas that figure for 1962 was down to about 40 per cent. This was not due to an absolute decline in the value of these food exports, but to the increases in bauxite and manufactured products.[8]

Although it is true that a summary discussion of these indices of national economic growth and well-being shows outstanding accomplishments in recent years, it is also true that there have not been significant improvements in the material standing of large segments of the population. Those persons with some advantage, whether it be capital, property, education, or skills, have gained most from the development of Jamaica's economy. Notably, the middle classes have received a considerable share of the increased income. This served to increase the balance of payments problem by stimulating imports of consumer goods and tended to limit capital formation by local saving.[9]

The share of wages in the urban sector has diminished in recent years while the total company profits have been increasing. Only slight increases in agricultural income have occurred. Also, unemployment and underemployment remain a serious challenge, and will be even more acute now that the United Kingdom has imposed restrictions on immigration. The Jamaican government has estimated that if emigration ceases, the labor force will grow to 860,000 persons by 1970. This would require the creation of 182,000 new jobs between 1960 and 1970, just to hold unemployment down to the 1960 level of 13 per cent.[10] In the urban parish of Kingston nearly one fifth of the labor force was

[7] See *Five Year Independence Plan, op. cit.*, pp. 12–17.
[8] *Ibid.*, p. 21.
[9] *Economic Survey, Jamaica, 1960*, Central Planning Unit, Government of Jamaica, 1961, p. 3.
[10] *Economic Survey, Jamaica, 1961*, p. 27; and *National Accounts, 1961*, pp. 9–12.

unemployed in 1960, and one report indicates that more than half of the unemployed in all Jamaica at the time of the 1960 census were living in the Kingston-St. Andrew metropolitan parishes.[11] Even these figures may underestimate the real nature of unemployment and the number of new jobs to be provided because the 1960 figures are based on the census taken in April, a month of unusually full employment. Recent estimates suggest that if the enumeration had been done in August, the number of unemployed would have increased by about 10,000 to total over 90,000 persons or about 14 per cent of the labor force.[12] Of course, underemployment and various forms of concealed unemployment are also significant problems which further aggravate the labor situation.

Like most of the West Indian territories, Jamaica has a very unequal distribution of land under cultivation. Figures for 1961 indicate that 56 per cent of the acreage was in 1,130 farms of 100 or more acres. At the other extreme, 113,239 farms accounted for 12 per cent of the acreage.[13] As shown in Table 4, it also appears that since 1954 there

Table 4. PERCENTAGE DISTRIBUTION OF FARMS BY SIZE AND ACREAGE IN EACH SIZE GROUP, 1954 and 1961*

Size	Per Cent of Farms 1954	Per Cent of Acreage 1954	Per Cent of Farms 1961	Per Cent of Acreage 1961
500 or more acres	0.2	40.0	0.2	45.3
100–500 acres	0.5	11.4	0.5	10.6
25–99 acres	2.4	10.8	2.4	9.4
5–24 acres	23.7	23.9	25.6	22.9
0–4 acres	73.2	13.9	71.3	11.8
	100.0	100.0	100.0	100.0
	(189,906)	(1,788,660)	(158,941)	(1,706,560)

* Computed from figures given in the Jamaican Government's *Five Year Independence Plan, 1963–1968*, Kingston: The Government Printer, 1963, p. 17.

has been an increasing amalgamation of farm holdings. These figures give some idea of the structure of agriculture in Jamaica and will serve as a background against which the trend of migration to urban centers must be viewed.

In general, Jamaica has moved to politically independent status with

---
[11] *Five Year Independence Plan, 1963–1968*, Kingston: The Government Printer, 1963, p. 36. See also O. C. Francis, *The People of Modern Jamaica*, Jamaica: Department of Statistics, 1963, pp. 7, 23–24.
[12] *Ibid.*, p. 33.
[13] *Ibid.*, p. 17.

a remarkable record of economic growth, especially in the 1950's. It surpassed the rates of economic growth achieved in the Latin American countries and it has been favorably compared with Japan and Puerto Rico. In addition, projections for future growth seem to be favorable, particularly in the manufacturing sector.[14] It is also true that the economy of Jamaica, like many relatively small developing countries, is subject to the fluctuating needs and tastes of foreign markets, and to the vagaries of foreign capital investment. In the context of these factors, Jamaica is attempting to come to a satisfactory solution to the problem of maintaining its economic growth rate and providing the increased services and amenities demanded by a modernizing population. As the Government's *Five Year Independence Plan* states, "The Jamaican situation is a classic demonstration of the race between development and discontent." The question which this implies is whether Jamaica can continue to rely on its combination of private enterprise and democratic politics.

Who are Jamaicans? Jamaican society has been called a potpourri in recognition of the many racial and national groups that make up its population. In addition to the large majority of Africans there are small but significant groups of Chinese, East Indians, Lebanese, Jews, Portuguese, and people from the British Isles as well as a large segment of colored persons of mixed descent. In spite of this diverse conglomeration, the population of Jamaica is relatively homogeneous. Black-skinned people of African descent made up three quarters of the population in 1960, and another 15 per cent were Afro-European.[15] This composition has changed little since 1884 when 95 per cent of the population were classified as black or colored.[16]

Marked social differentiation, however, exists in Jamaica. In addition to race and color, important differences in economic position and institutional practices are the basis of a highly stratified society. Examination of the occupational distribution of male heads of households who were wage earners in 1960 gives some indication of the economic basis of Jamaican social structure:[17]

---

[14] For example see *The New York Times*, August 5, 1962, Section 11, p. 5; *Trade Indices*, 1948–1962, *op. cit.*, p. 9.

[15] *West Indies Population Census, 1960*, Bulletin No. 20 (Provisional) Kingston: Department of Statistics, 1962, p. 1.

[16] George W. Roberts, *The Population of Jamaica*, Cambridge: University Press, 1957, p. 65.

[17] These data are from the *West Indies Population Census, 1960*, Kingston, Jamaica: Department of Statistics, as adapted by James T. Duke, "Equalitarianism Among Emergent Elites in a New Nation," unpublished Ph.D. dissertation, University of California, Los Angeles, Calif., 1963.

Professionals	0.6 per cent
Managers and officials	6.7
Clerical and sales	6.8
Skilled manual and service	23.6
Unskilled manual and service	62.2
Total	99.9 per cent
Number	(258,220)

These differences in occupation, and those in income, education, and landownership, are both causes and consequences of positions of social and economic dominance in Jamaica, and they are quite clearly correlated with variations in institutional or subcultural forms. Race, color, kinship institutions, religious practices, property concepts, work organization, and economic institutions are among the many dimensions of social differentiation which mark Jamaican society.[18] Moreover, these differences are highly correlated with one another as might be expected. The most extreme differences in Jamaican social structure are between the white upper class and the black lower classes. This historically determined social and economic cleavage between the black masses and the white and light skinned upper strata may be clearly seen in the distribution of occupations by race and color. An approximation to this correlation between color and occupation is shown in the following information from the 1943 Census on the occupational distribution of male wage earners and unpaid workers by color:[19]

Occupation	Black	Brown	White
Managers and Officials	0.1%	1.9%	20.4%
Professionals	0.6	2.6	13.8
Clerical and Sales	2.1	14.9	31.5
Skilled manual and skilled service	15.6	27.3	20.2
Unskilled manual and unskilled service	81.6	53.3	14.1
Total	100.0%	100.0%	100.0%
Number of cases	(162,554)	(31,225)	(2,495)

The correlation between color and occupation is probably underestimated for 1943 because these data do not include employers or "own account" workers. But since the data are twenty years old (more recent figures are unavailable), caution must be exercised in

---

[18] See M. G. Smith, "The Plural Framework of Jamaican Society," *The British Journal of Sociology*, XII (September, 1961), pp. 249–262.
[19] These data are drawn from the *Eighth Census of Jamaica and Its Dependencies, 1943*, as adapted by James T. Duke, op. cit.

applying them to Jamaica today. I would suggest that the trend of change since 1943 would have included more black, and certainly more brown persons in the higher occupations, but the overall relationship would be little affected.

These same data discussed above can also be presented in a fashion which allows a clearer answer to the question, "What percentage of the persons in each of these occupational groups are black, brown, or white?" This is shown in the following color distribution of male wage earners and unpaid workers by occupational classification:[20]

Occupation	Black	Brown	White	Totals	(Number of Cases)
Managers and officials	12.9%	46.9%	40.2%	100.0%	(1,265)
Professionals	45.8	38.1	16.1	100.0	(2,131)
Clerical and sales	38.5	52.6	8.9	100.0	(8,852)
Skilled manual and skilled service	73.7	24.8	1.5	100.0	(34,386)
Unskilled manual and unskilled service	88.6	11.1	0.3	100.0	(149,640)
Per cent of the total	82.8	15.9	1.3	100.0	(196,274)

Again, these data should be approached with caution since they are based on the 1943 census, and do not include the total labor force. One of the striking figures in the foregoing table is the relatively high percentage of professionals who are black. This is perhaps most clearly interpreted as a commentary on the importance of education in structuring opportunities for social mobility in Jamaica.

A similar correlation existed between color and income in 1943. Two per cent of the white wage earners and 58 per cent of the black wage earners received less than 10 shillings per week. Less than 1 per cent of the black wage earners had an income of more than 100 shillings per week compared to 41 per cent of the whites whose income exceeded that level.[21] This inequity in the distribution of incomes in Jamaica was in 1961–62 the subject of considerable discussion. Making use of the "catchy and emotive phrase, 'the have and the have-nots'," Jamaica Labour Party politicians focused legislative debates and popular appeals on inequalities in the income distribution.[22] It was claimed that 93 per cent of the population were "have-nots" with incomes of less than £300 per annum. The validity of these figures was seriously questioned because of the use of income tax data and their combination with data from the National Accounts. G. E. Cumper of the University of the West Indies has estimated that 57 percent of all households

---

[20] Recomputed from the table presented by Duke, *ibid*.
[21] *Ibid*.
[22] *The West Indian Economist*, III (May, 1961), pp. 4–7.

in Jamaica in 1958 had incomes of less than £300 per annum.[23] He also has noted, from a sample survey of household expenditures in Kingston in 1954, that those households with weekly incomes of less than £2 accounted for 30 per cent of all households, while 15 per cent had incomes of £15 per week.[24] Whatever the inaccuracies of these income distribution estimates it is clear that marked inequities existed.

Income and prestige are correlated with employment patterns, and the occupational recruitment system is based on the system of differential education. These intercorrelations suggest the importance of educational opportunities as the basis of social stratification in Jamaica. This has been augmented by the increased importance of education in recent years as a means of social mobility.[25]

Writing of the striking correlation between race, income, and residential location in Kingston, Blanshard observed,

> The residential sections of the suburbs rise gradually toward the Blue Mountains, and as they rise the temperature falls about one degree for each hundred feet of elevation, the income rises about $500 a year, and the racial complexion of the residents changes with the elevation.[26]

This summary discussion of Jamaican social structure and the nature of the island-society's social differentiation has emphasized the correlated social and economic cleavages and points of poor social integration. The literature on underdeveloped societies contains many comments on the existence and importance of such cleavages along several dimensions of social structure. David A. Wilson has noted that such "gaps" may be the result of the process of modernization.[27] I would suggest that these correlated cleavages which characterize Jamaican social structure have been present in more or less the same form

---

[23] This estimate was prepared in 1962 by G. E. Cumper, Institute of Social and Economic Research, University of the West Indies.

[24] G. E. Cumper, "Personal Consumption in the West Indies," in Cumper (ed.), *The Economy of the West Indies,* Kingston: Institute of Social and Economic Research, University College of the West Indies, by United Printers, Ltd., 1960, p. 127.

[25] See M. G. Smith, *op. cit.,* pp. 252–254. While I have used the term "class" to refer to the hierarchically arranged social aggregates in Jamaica, Smith prefers to call them cultural or social "sections." Concerning education as a means of social mobility in Jamaica, see his "Education and Occupational Choice in Rural Jamaica," *Social and Economic Studies,* 9 (September, 1960), p. 351.

[26] Paul Blanshard, *Democracy and Empire in the Caribbean,* New York: The Macmillan Company, 1947, pp. 86–87.

[27] David A. Wilson, "Nation-Building and Revolutionary War," in Karl Deutsch and William J. Foltz (editors), *Nation-Building,* New York: Atherton Press, 1963, p. 87.

throughout most of its history, and further, that the process of modernization has probably served to reduce their importance to some extent. For example, while the monetary gap between the rich and the poor may have increased, the minimums of income have also risen, and greater numbers of people have become meaningful participants in the economy. Rising minimums of social and political rights have had similar integrative effects. The next section discusses these changes in more detail.

A GENERAL FRAMEWORK OF SOCIAL TRENDS

The history of change in Jamaica, including the more recent modernizing years, has been interpreted as a long term trend of increases in the scale of society. Bell has given the following description of that trend:

> Jamaica represents, at least since discovery and probably before that, a society which has been expanding in people, in degree of organization and complexity, in total power and wealth, in equality and internal inclusiveness, in space, and in time.[28]

These increases in the number of people in interaction and interdependence, the expansion of communication in time and space, and the heightened participation of Jamaicans in all processes of the society are increases in the scale of society.[29] The processes of industrial development, urbanization, and the related increases in technology, education, literacy, transportation and communication have served to increase the range of social relations of Jamaicans with the rest of the world as well as internally. We shall be concerned here with the internal processes rather than with the increasing scope of Jamaica's international relations.[30]

One critically important aspect of expanding scale of Jamaican society has been the process of increasing internal inclusiveness and the spread of equality. The lessening of hereditary privilege and the

---

[28] Wendell Bell, *Jamaican Leaders: Political Attitudes in a New Nation*, Berkeley and Los Angeles: University of California Press, 1964, p. 33. See also his "Social Change and Elites in an Emergent Nation," Chapter 7 in Herbert R. Barringer, George I. Blanksten, and Raymond W. Mack (editors), *Social Change in Underdeveloped Areas: A Reinterpretation of Evolutionary Theory*, Cambridge, Mass.: Schenkman Publishing Co., 1965.

[29] See Godfrey and Monica Wilson, *The Analysis of Social Change*, Cambridge: University Press, 1954; and Eshref Shevky and Wendell Bell, *Social Area Analysis*, Stanford University Press, 1955, pp. 3–19.

[30] For a discussion of the increases in external or international interaction of Jamaica see Charles C. Moskos, Jr., and Wendell Bell, "Emergent Caribbean Nations Face the Outside World," *Social Problems*, 12 (Summer, 1964), pp. 24–41; see also Bell, *Jamaican Leaders*, Chapter VII.

reduction of other ascriptive barriers which limited social participation and interaction in traditional Jamaica have been significant features of change. Gradually, Jamaica has been moving toward the provision of equal opportunities for the utilization of the society's facilities, services, and resources. One of the most powerful forces in the modern world, nationalism, emerged in the West Indies as a consequence of this drive toward the establishment of egalitarian societies, as demonstrated by Moskos in his study of nationalist attitudes among West Indian leaders.[31] The sequence of constitutional advances and the spread of equality which culminated in national independence have served to minimize the rigid "status immobility" and "civil immobility" which were restricting social and political participation.[32]

The spread of equality as a major social trend of Jamaican society has been documented by Bell. Focusing on the long term trends of change rather than on cycles or fluctuations, he has argued that in Jamaican history since the fifteenth century the spread of equality may be seen in the continued extension of rising minimums of human rights for an increasing proportion of the Jamaican people. Human rights were defined according to the United Nations' usage of that conception to include civil, political, economic, and social and cultural rights.[33] Historic acts of the Jamaican Assembly and the British Parliament regarding the rights of Africans brought to Jamaica and their descendants, and more recently, the provision of educational facilities for the mass of Jamaicans, the changing social composition of Jamaican elites, the introduction of universal adult suffrage, and the subsequent high level of popular political participation are ready illustrations of these changes.[34]

In accepting Bell's interpretation of the social history of Jamaica, it must certainly be acknowledged, as he does, that Jamaica today is a society characterized by marked inequality. However, the inequities in human rights were clearly more extreme in the past. Some of the remaining inequalities were mentioned in our earlier discussion of

---

[31] Charles C. Moskos, Jr., *The Sociology of Political Independence: A Study of Nationalist Attitudes Among West Indian Leaders*, Cambridge, Mass.: Schenkman Publishing Co., 1967.

[32] David A. Wilson writes of segments of a population being immobilized by underemployment, lack of political participation, castes, and superstitions. See his discussion of "Nation-Building and Revolutionary War," *op. cit.*, pp. 87–88.

[33] Bell, *Jamaican Leaders*, pp. 33–49.

[34] On the changing composition of elites see Leonard Broom, "The Social Differentiation of Jamaica," *American Sociological Review*, 19 (April, 1954), pp. 124–125; and Bell, *Jamaican Leaders*, Chapter III. In the General Election of 1962, 72.88 per cent of the 796,540 registered voters exercised their right to vote; *Report of the Chief Electoral Officer, General Election, 1962*, p. 4.

Jamaican social structure. Presently, there are gross inequalities of opportunity and access to the means for achieving one's social, economic, and political objectives. But these facts do not negate the contention regarding the long term trend of increasing equality.

URBANIZATION AND THE SLUMS

Another important aspect of Jamaica's increasing scale has been the process of urbanization, and in particular the growth of the urban lower classes. The island's total population increased by 30 per cent between the census of 1943 and that of 1960, but the growth in the Kingston Metropolitan Area far outstripped the island-wide figure. The population of Urban St. Andrew and the parish of Kingston, the territory referred to as the Metropolitan Area, increased from 203,000 to 379,000 persons, an increase of 87 per cent. The greatest part of this increase took place in Urban St. Andrew where the population rose from 93,000 to 254,000 persons, an increase of 173 per cent. The density of this area was recorded as 1,646 persons per square mile. The other major towns of Jamaica showed high increases also.[35]

These changes in the distribution of the island's population are reflected historically in the increasing importance of Kingston as a commercial, industrial, and administrative center. Kingston has become the distribution center for Jamaica because of the importance of its imports and the increased consumption of imported goods in recent years. Comparison of cargo tonnage handled in 1952 shows that 97 per cent of all imports by tonnage were unloaded at Kingston, while only 26 per cent of the exports were handled there. On the average since 1952, nearly 80 per cent of all cargo tonnage of imports have been discharged at Kingston.[36] As Maunder has noted, this has been influential in the pattern of industrial development. Of the government Industrial Development Corporation and the incentive legislation which has been passed, he wrote, "All these measures apply to the Island as a whole, but their short-run effects are likely to be of greatest significance to Kingston, the seat of light industry."[37] The result has been what the Prime Minister bemoaned as the "daily flocking . . . into Kingston seeking non-existent employment."[38]

The move to the cities began in large numbers in 1911 by which time there was little remaining farm land for resettlement. This early

---

[35] *Economic Survey, Jamaica, 1961*, p. 23.
[36] W. F. Maunder, *Employment in an Underdeveloped Area*, New Haven: Yale University Press, 1960, p. 60. For figures for the years 1952–62, see *Annual Abstract of Statistics, 1962*, No. 22, Kingston: Department of Statistics, 1964, p. 53.
[37] Maunder, *op. cit.*, p. 62.
[38] *Spotlight*, XXIV (March, 1963), p. 10.

urban growth was to have great significance for the future of Jamaica. The violent disturbances of 1938 must be interpreted in the light of this migration. As Cumper has written:

> ... life in the city was insecure, particularly in the early years of urban expansion, when even such amenities as sewers and police patrols were lacking in the new working class suburbs. The government which faced these problems was administratively superior to that which failed in 1865, but it was hampered in its attempts to deal with these half-realized tensions by the powerful representation it gave to local conservative interests, including merchants who objected both on principle and interest to any extension of government responsibility for the expenditure on working class welfare.[39]

Jamaica is quite typical of developing countries in the inability of its urban areas to absorb the increased numbers and in the resulting concentrations of unemployed, the vast numbers of sub-standard houses, and the generally inferior services and facilities. The trend of internal migration has not slackened, nor have there been any effective attempts to deal with the more evident problems of the growing urban lower class in their ghetto-like world.

Almost twenty years ago Professor T. S. Simey, commenting on these conditions, suggested that the colonies of the West Indies and the British Empire at large could only be ashamed of the plight of the unemployed and unemployable proletariat. He said that the problem of clearing Kingston's slums was insoluble, and "There was in 1945 no sign that anything better could be accomplished in the future."[40] Although one cannot agree that nothing *could be* accomplished, it is true that little or nothing was done. In this respect Professor Simey's prediction was accurate. Witness this more recent commentary.

> The slums of Kingston are beyond description. Even the camera glamorises them, except in shots taken from the air. Hovels of board and cardboard and canvas and tin lie choked together on damp rubbish dumps behind which the sun sets in mocking splendour. More respectable and on drier ground are the packing-case houses, the tiniest houses ever built, suggesting a vast arrested community given over to playing in grubby dolls' houses. Then there are the once real houses packed to the bursting point, houses so close in streets so narrow that there is no feeling of openness. Filth and rubbish are disgorged everywhere. . . . And wherever you look you see the surrounding Kingston hills, one of the beauties of the island. . . . Against such a view lay a dead mule, its

---

[39] G. E. Cumper, "Population Movements in Jamaica, 1830–1950," *Social and Economic Studies*, V (September, 1956), p. 274.
[40] T. S. Simey, *Welfare and Planning in the West Indies*, Oxford: The Clarendon Press, 1946, pp. 228–229.

teeth bared, its belly swollen and taut. It had been there for two days; a broomstick had been playfully stuck in its anus.[41]

This novelist's commentary has been rejected by many Jamaicans as hogwash. Unfortunately, their attitude is an emotional reaction rather than one based on knowledge and awareness.

The contrasts in Kingston were no less dramatically portrayed by a British social scientist who attributed Jamaica's urban growth to both prosperity and destitution — to the growing middle classes riding the crest of economic advancement, and the burgeoning urban masses who had fled from the frustration of the rural areas.

> The top groups have climbed up to new suburbs. . . . Down below, the dreadful shack dumps of West Kingston have become darker, denser, larger. . . . The sights, the smells, the sounds, even the forces of heat and rain, are those of a different world. Here there are flimsy miserable huts, thrown together, made of refuse — paper, cardboard, packing cases, bits of sticks, and parts of discarded motor-car bodies. . . . The Kingston jungles are exceptional both in the extent and in the degree of abandonment they expose.[42]

It is not surprising that such commentary has been largely rejected by Jamaicans. It is not pleasant. It scars the face that Jamaica presents to the prospective investor, to the tourist, to the world. But behind this ethnocentric pride there is a more significant and disturbing reason for the rejection of these descriptions of West Kingston. I speak of the antipathy, the distaste, and more commonly, the indifference toward the growing urban lower classes.[43]

Responsible persons are aware of the threat these attitudes may hold for the future of Jamaica. They have been advocating a change in the thinking of middle and upper class Jamaicans toward the people of West Kingston. A West Kingston pastor has asked the privileged classes ". . . to become aware of the conditions in the lives of these people, and to become willing to face the problem as a national issue."[44] Similarly, a government research sociologist working in West Kingston wondered ". . . how long despair and hopelessness can be contained." He said further, "Whether other people like the underprivi-

---

[41] V. S. Naipaul, *The Middle Passage*, London: Andre Deutsch, Ltd., 1962, p. 216.
[42] Ruth Glass, "Ashes of Discontent: The Past As Present in Jamaica," *Monthly Review*, XIV (May, 1962), pp. 26–27.
[43] The leaders interviewed in this study were asked to describe the typical attitude of middle and upper-class Jamaicans toward the urban lower classes. Nearly half of the respondents stated that the majority attitude was one of apathy or indifference. Thirty-seven per cent said the typical attitude was that of antipathy.
[44] *Spotlight*, XXIV (March, 1963), p. 17.

leged or don't like them, here they are. Their condition and the indifference of others to them constitute a peril that might erupt at any time."⁴⁵

In general, more Jamaicans are becoming aware of the masses and their importance in Jamaica's future. As urbanization has progressed and the scale of society increased, the growing urban masses have intruded more and more in the social reality that is Jamaica. The urban lower classes have become increasingly a part of the image of Jamaican society held by the dominant or privileged classes. The significance of the masses has been more clearly realized as they have impinged more strongly upon the consciousness of the middle and upper classes. Following Hoetink's analysis, I suggest that the masses have become "real" in the societal image held by the dominant group; that is, the masses have come to provoke the notion of menace in the subjective conception held by the privileged classes.⁴⁶

The expanding scale, the spread of equality and the increasing internal inclusiveness of Jamaican society have underscored the remaining contradictions in Jamaican social structure. These trends of change have served to emphasize the critical significance of the growing urban lower classes for the future of Jamaica.

⁴⁵ *Spotlight*, XXII (October–November, 1961), p. 12.
⁴⁶ H. Hoetink, "Changes in Prejudice," *Bijdragen Tot De Taal-, Land-, en Volkenkunde*, Deel 119 (1963), pp. 65–66.

CHAPTER 3 Images of the Future

Images of the future are expectations about the state of things to come at some future time. Such images of the future that are held by a nation's leaders, particularly their expectations regarding their nation's potential, are critically important as they go about making decisions of nationhood because of the numerous aspects of change that are amenable to history-making decisions. In this chapter, images of Jamaica's future held by public leaders in Jamaica are described and compared with the images of the future held by the urban lower classes, and some cross-national comparisons are also made.

The basic data of the study were collected in interviews completed with a sample of 54 persons drawn from a systematically defined universe of Jamaican leaders. These leaders included Members of Parliament, Cabinet Ministers, high-ranking civil servants, heads of major community organizations, elected local politicians, religious leaders, and several prominent barristers, solicitors, and businessmen. These leaders were selected from a universe of leaders defined by reputational or "power attribution" methods as persons who were powerful in spheres of decision-making and in the formulation and implementation of policy concerning West Kingston and its people. (The details of these procedures and other methodology, including the interview schedule, are discussed more fully in the Appendices.)

Four questions were asked of the Jamaican leaders to discover their images of the future of the new nation. They were worded so that the leaders could discuss any aspect of the nation's future that they were interested in and to which they gave highest priority. The questions were designed to elicit the leaders' visions of future developments with the respondents themselves providing the terms of the discussion and choosing the aspects of the future they wanted to stress. In the order in which they were asked, these questions proceeded from the general to the specific, as presented in Table 5. The first question referred to the future of the island-nation most broadly; the second dealt with the expected effects of political independence upon the nation; and the last

Table 5. PERCENTAGE DISTRIBUTION OF JAMAICAN LEADERS ACCORDING TO THEIR RESPONSES TO FOUR QUESTIONS ABOUT THE FUTURE

1. "Generally, do you think the people of Jamaica will be better off, about the same, or worse off after independence (that is, in the future)?"

	Per Cent
Better off	61
About the same	4
Worse off	35
Total	100
Number of cases	(54)

2. "Do you think that independence itself will make any difference?"

Yes, for the better	38
No	48
Uncertain	6
Yes, for the worse	8
Total	100
Number of cases	(52)
No answer	(2)

3. "With particular reference to that area [Western Kingston], do you expect any significant changes to take place after independence (that is, in the future)?"

Yes, for the better	44
No	40
Uncertain	2
Yes, for the worse	14
Total	100
Number of cases	(50)
No answer	(4)

4. "A few people have told me that some form of civil disorder or violent outbreak is likely to arise out of West Kingston. Do you think it is likely?"

No, not likely at all	40
No, but possible	26
Uncertain	4
Yes	30
Total	100
Number of cases	(50)
No answer	(4)

two questions specifically asked about the respondents' images of the future of West Kingston, whose 100,000 residents had become, as discussed earlier, the symbol of the most important social problems facing the newly independent country.

The leaders were prepared for the generality of these questions by the question that preceded those on images of the future. This earlier question queried them about the trends of change from 1938 to the present. The year 1938, more than any other, had marked the beginning of the development of modern political consciousness among the Jamaican people, and the events of that year started the drive which was to culminate in the achievement of independence. Having just evaluated these changes wrought upon the economy, polity, and society in the recent past, the leaders generally were prepared to project their thoughts into the new era marked by independence. In fact, several respondents anticipated the questions about the future.

On the first question about Jamaica's future progress, the leaders were quite optimistic in their views, with 61 per cent contemplating a favorable future, 4 per cent suggesting that things would be about the same, and 35 per cent saying that the Jamaican people would be worse off. Looking at the responses to the second question, one can see whether the changes resulting from independence provided the basis for the beliefs revealed in the replies to the first question. Forty-eight per cent of the leaders foresaw no significant effects from independence, while 8 per cent anticipated deleterious consequences. Thirty-eight per cent of the leaders thought independence was likely to give favorable impetus to Jamaica's development. Thus, among these leaders, favorable images of Jamaica's future were in the majority, but only part of this optimism was based on the advent of independence. That is, some leaders foresaw a favorable national future irrespective of the political transition to independence.

When asked about the future of West Kingston, the leaders' images of the future were less favorable than those for the island as a whole. Forty-four per cent of the leaders anticipated a more favorable future for the lower-class area, while 14 per cent predicted further deterioration. The next largest group of 40 per cent expected no changes in the area. Given the conditions in the west side of Kingston in 1961–62, I would conclude that because there is so much room for improvement, the expectation of no change amounts to consigning the area and its people to everlasting deprivation. Recalling that these respondents are all in some sense community welfare leaders whose interests and responsibilities lie in some measure with the betterment of West Kingston, the reader may well conclude that the figure of 40 per cent expecting no change in the area is an unfortunate finding, particularly when thought of as a statement of futility and impotence. Further, designating this answer as unfavorable is consistent with Polak's definition of favorable images of the future as those which optimistically anticipate a radically different and infinitely better state of affairs to come.[1] The favorable image of the future characterized by an idealistic vision of future progress is not to be found in expectations of things to remain as they are, at least in West Kingston.

[1] Fred L. Polak, *The Image of the Future: Enlightening the Past, Orienting the Present, Forecasting the Future*, translated by Elise Boulding, Leyden, Netherlands: A. W. Sythoff, New York: Oceana Publications, 1961, I, p. 58.

The last question in Table 5 is somewhat different and more specific than the preceding questions. Is violent civil disorder thought to be likely? The relevance of this aspect of the future to this research and these leaders was underscored by the frequent discussions, both during formal interviews and in the preliminary research, of the likelihood of outbreaks of violence in West Kingston. Many anxious and worried comments about the possibility of violent disturbances were made by the leaders at some point in the interview prior to my question on the subject. Consciousness of these possibilities probably grew in part from a general awareness of discontent among lower-class people, and growing black racist sentiments, in addition to an alleged attempt to incite Ras Tafari cultists to armed violence. The Ras Tafari brethren are a heterogeneous collection of Jamaicans, mostly poor and black, who believe that Ras Tafari, the Emperor Haile Selassie of Ethiopia, is the living God. Further, they believe that salvation for the black man can come only by means of repatriation to Africa. They have rejected the "brown man's government" and any attempts it has made to help them, with the slogan "We want repatriation, not rehabilitation." Although the problems symbolized by the "rastas" are certainly significant, Afro-oriented groups such as this have not had much political impact.

Early in the summer of 1960, Claudius V. Henry, a self-styled religious leader of the cult, recently returned from the United States, and several of his followers were arrested for possession of an arsenal of firearms, gunpowder, and explosives. In addition to the confiscation of these weapons, the alleged discovery of documents linking the group with Cuban and American subversive backing resulted in charges of treason being brought against Henry and some of his followers. In June 1960, another group was captured in the hills to the west of Kingston where two British soldiers and three Ras Tafari brethren had been killed earlier. These incidents and the courts of inquiry and trials which followed received widespread coverage in the island's mass media. The publicity given to these incidents, and to the threat of extremists, and Ras Tafari brethren and Communists, rekindled old fears of many Jamaicans.[2] In the summer of 1962, these incidents of two years earlier were very often referred to by the Jamaican leaders interviewed.

[2] The background of these incidents and the developments in the months that followed are discussed in detail in the Jamaican news magazines, *Newday*, IV (May, August, 1960), and *Spotlight*, XXI (June, July, August, 1960). See also the Jamaican newspaper, *The Daily Gleaner*, for that period. The letters to the editor displayed an interesting range of attitudes and reactions to these incidents. These occurrences are also discussed in Katrin Norris, *Jamaica: The Search for an Identity*, London: Oxford University Press for the Institute of Race Relations, 1962, pp. 49–51. See also M. G. Smith, Roy Augier, and Rex Nettleford, *The Ras Tafari Movement in Kingston, Jamaica*, Kingston: University College of the West Indies, 1960.

When asked about the likelihood of violent disturbances in the future, 40 per cent of the leaders thought such occurrences were not likely at all, and many scoffed at the suggestion that such civil disorder was to be expected. But 56 per cent of the leaders said that such an incident was either likely or possible. One of the more frenetic politicians said:

> It's inescapable. I hear them talk. They don't care for man or God. And they're sure not going to care what they do to the man up top. I think some sort of civil disturbance is impossible to avoid, and right now . . . the security of the individual is at a low ebb. . . . Even the police walk in fear down here.

Another respondent, a clergyman working in West Kingston, said the pressure was building up in the area and the lid was likely to blow off.

None of these leaders indicated that they would favor violent civil disorder as a potential lever for change. Expectations of such disorder were viewed as an unfavorable prediction, while the belief that such occurrences were *not* likely was taken as a favorable prediction about the future.

ELABORATION OF THE IMAGES OF JAMAICA'S FUTURE

Because the responses to the above questions (Table 5) constitute a central part of this research, and because most of the later analysis will focus on the evaluative character of the responses and not on the specific content of the leaders' images of the future, some attention should be given here to how and why the leaders viewed the future as better or worse than the present. Some elaboration of the detailed content of the leaders' discussions of Jamaica's future should give additional meaning to the analysis to follow, and will convey some of the flavor and essence of their outlooks.

Looking first at only those leaders who expressed favorable images of the island-nation's future, we see that there was considerable variation in the ways in which they depicted the future as being better than the present. Nearly two thirds of them based their optimism on the belief that the Jamaican economy would improve. Such views included the prediction that economic growth would continue with, among other things, increased access to foreign markets and increased capital through more loans and grants. Expectations of gross economic growth were mentioned by the leaders nearly twice as frequently as improvements in wages, levels of living, and the extent to which the "small man" was to share the nation's economic success. Perhaps the leaders assumed that these distributional improvements would follow as a matter of course. Even if this were true, it was somewhat surprising that mass participation of the population in the future advances of the economy was not mentioned by more than 30 per cent of these leaders, since during this time there was much publicity given to Jamaica's "haves and have-nots"[3] and since all of these leaders were persons who bore some responsibility for dealing with one of the most economically depressed areas of the society.

Concentrating still on those leaders who reported favorable images of the future for the island in general, we find that nearly two thirds of these leaders anticipated favorable changes in the broad social features of the island. Most frequently mentioned was the rise of a Jamaican identity, which included the growth of a nationalist spirit and awareness of social responsibilities. For example, one respondent predicted the development ". . . of willingness of people to meet the sacrifices and accept the responsibilities that will be necessary if independence is to be a success." A steady trend of improvement was depicted by another respondent who said:

> Jamaica will continue to move forward with no rapid change for the better or the worse. We're likely to move forward because Jamaica has now become a more sober country since last year. People don't have the gambling-boom complex and will be satisfied with less. The change of government has helped to sober the people so that in the future they are less inclined to think that the government will represent a source of magic that will, like the wave of a wand, solve all problems.

Another frequently mentioned social aspect was a future society marked by increased internal inclusiveness and fewer barriers to mobility and opportunity, the extension of civil liberties and human rights, and increased availability of education and social services. The following illustrates this expectation:

> As a society and community of people, Jamaica is going to be much better off with more stability and more cohesion. The basic cleavages we now have in our society are based on the economy and the educational system. I say this for the following reasons: Our stratification in Jamaica is most clearly based on economics, and the economics of Jamaica, personal economics that is, are based completely on education. Therefore, we'll become a more cohesive society with stratification reduced as education becomes more widespread and the opportunities for good education made more equal.

The literature on new nations might lead one to expect many references to political-developmental problems by Jamaican leaders in their

---

[3] "Jamaica's Income and Its Distribution," *The West Indian Economist*, III (May, 1961), pp. 4–7.

explanations of their images of the future. But, among those who held favorable views of the future, political developments were seldom mentioned as ways in which the nation's future would be better than the present. Almost 60 per cent of the leaders who saw a favorable future did *not* refer to politics in describing Jamaica's future. An explanation of this finding can be offered from the history of Jamaican political development. The relatively long period of tutelage during which the United Kingdom bore final responsibility for governing the territory created the conditions for the development of political structures, institutions, and experience adequate for independence. The slow constitutional development and the gradual movement toward self-government and fully local responsibility over the years since 1944, coupled with the creation of an independent civil service, have removed much of the political process as an area of concern or threat to the nation's future. In the eyes of many Jamaicans, the realization of these achievements has left little room for improvement. Perhaps it is this sense of accomplishment which is reflected in the infrequency of references to the political sphere in the leaders' images of the future. In their view, political development had been achieved and political rights had been granted to all. What remained as a primary task for the nation was the extension of social and economic rights and opportunities to all Jamaicans.

Turning now to the content of the unfavorable images of the future as presented by the minority of leaders interviewed, one finds that the distribution of concern with problems of the economy, polity, and society, in general, was similar to that of the leaders who anticipated future progress. Among those who were pessimistic about the general future of their society, we find again that somewhat less than half of the leaders referred to fears concerning politics. And among these responses, about equal emphasis was given to expectations of corrupt, incompetent government and instability of the two-party parliamentary democracy as was given to immature and unwise political behavior on the part of the Jamaican electorate. Generally, dire predictions for Jamaica's future were based on problems other than those involving political institutions or the political process.

Three quarters of those leaders who portrayed Jamaica as having a doubtful future anticipated a failure of economic development programs, declining levels of capital investment, more severe competition in foreign markets, and the depression of manufacturing and agricultural production. Such problems for the national economy were the most frequent reasons given for a gloomy prediction.

Undesirable social developments were mentioned by 71 per cent of the leaders who were doubtful about their national future. The majority of these pessimistic respondents were highly critical of the Jamaican masses. Lack of pride, discipline, unity, oneness of purpose, and the failure of great numbers of Jamaicans to accept family responsibilities were commonly attributed to the average Jamaican. Almost a fourth of the pessimistic leaders also based their misgivings about the future on Malthusian fears for the island's numbers. Many of these dealt with problems of emigration and population distribution as well as control of the vital rates.

The following quotations from the interviews exhibit several of these facets of the doubtful future better than can be conveyed in a statistical description.

> It depends on a lot of imponderables. Firstly, unless the economy can be maintained at a growth rate of approximately 5 to 7 per cent at constant prices, plus a sizeable migration of 15 to 20 thousand persons per year, unemployment will increase, the economy will suffer, and there will be a greater strain on social services. Secondly, who knows what the outflow of population might be? . . . A lot will depend on how this outflow is maintained. A lot will also depend on how England's economy grows and on Jamaica's access to development funds. . . . Thirdly, who can predict how much aid will come from the United States and this depends to a great extent upon the cleverness of our government. Taking all these things into consideration, I think we have a few long tough years ahead and Jamaica is facing a tough time.

A dark future for Jamaica was clearly stated by a civil servant who said:

> In the future in general, say for the next 20 years, the process of change will have to continue if the expectations of the people are going to be fulfilled at all. The more disprivileged, or left-back groups will pressure for change to continue. . . . The fundamental relation of land and population will become more acute, and with migration drastically reduced, the size of the proletariat that is arising will increase continually. In addition, Jamaica will lose the protection of its Commonwealth connection. Sugar will go through a difficult period and many people will probably be squeezed out of employment as a result of the rationalization and mechanization in the sugar industry. . . . For the next ten years one couldn't be other than pessimistic. And who knows after that?

The leaders' explanations of their answers to the second question (Table 5), "Do you think that independence itself will make any difference?" further elaborate their images of the future. It was found that almost half of the leaders did not expect independence to have any significant effects on Jamaica's future progress. These were perhaps not unreasonable findings when one recalls the history of constitutional change and political development in Jamaica. Almost a quarter of a century intervened between the first stirrings of modern political consciousness in 1937–38, and the attainment of independence. This relatively long period of British tutelage and the gradualism which characterized Jamaican political change, although beneficial as a training period for democracy, seemed to vitiate the impact of independence itself. In this regard, one of the elected politicians responded:

> It's not a significant thing on a mass basis. It has come in small doses — like a man becoming accustomed to an antibiotic. He has been soaking it in. It came piecemeal. The Colonial Office and the Governors have never sought to take constitutional advantage of the elected politicians, so, since 1944, with the connivance of the officials, we have virtually had internal self-government at all times.

The essence of this leader's interpretation of Jamaican political development as the reason for the meager consequences of independence was echoed by 24 per cent of those leaders who expected independence to have little or no effect on the overall trend of Jamaica's development. This same line of reasoning regarding the gradual nature of political development was suggested earlier as an explanation of the infrequent references to political change in the leaders' images of Jamaica's future.

Another 10 per cent of those leaders who predicted that independence would have no effect indicated that the important future trends would have occurred regardless of independence. Independence alone was not an event that would greatly alter or accelerate the patterns of Jamaica's development.

Of greater interest is the fact that nearly two thirds of the leaders who said independence would have no effect gave reasons which were critical of the Jamaican people and their national leaders. For example, a civil servant of high standing reported that:

> The people who are in positions of leadership now are not facing up to the problem of public education. Trade unions, for example, are not facing up to this problem. Independence could be used as a catalyst. Independence could be used as a platform to say things that have never been said, but need to be. But, to my and other peoples' dismay, this is not being done.

Another comment, illustrative of the criticisms of the people and their leaders was supplied by a clergyman who said:

> There are people who have things happen to them, and people who make them happen. We are the former type. We've just been swept along without any long term emergent view. So, independence wasn't fought for and somewhere along the line we will have to pay the price. I don't know how much this price will be, or when we will be called upon to pay it, but I believe we will have to pay it because the people

do not understand the meaning of independence. If the people had a unity of purpose to make independence have some real meaning, then I think the people would be better off, and independence would be of some consequence.

This answer was implicitly critical of the leaders of the country for allowing Jamaica to be "swept along without a long term view," and for not leading the people into an understanding of the implications of independence. The masses were also criticized for not displaying the unity and cohesiveness which would enhance the favorable impact of independence. The most frequent reasons given for the lack of any consequences of the forthcoming independent status were reasons such as these.

Finally, there was a correlation between these reasons given for the inefficacy of independence and the expectations of a more favorable future in general. Of those leaders whose predictions of the ineffectiveness of independence were based upon conceptions critical of the Jamaican people and their leaders, 63 per cent saw the future in general as unfavorable, whereas only a third of those giving non-critical reasons based on the nature of recent political history held unfavorable images of the island's future.

DIFFERENTIAL IMAGES OF THE FUTURE: THE LEADERS AND THE LED

It has been suggested that people from different strata of society should be expected to hold differing views of the promise of the future. As Melvin Tumin and Arnold Feldman have noted, "Those who achieve better positions, whether by striving, advantage, or some combination of both, develop different sets of attitudes about future possibilities."[4]

Data collected in interviews with a sample of lower-class persons on the west side of Kingston allow some comparisons of their images of the future of the nation with those expressed by the Jamaican leaders. West Kingston was described in the preceding chapter as an area of lower-class residence which many Jamaicans view as the dumping ground of society. The rural areas pour many unskilled migrants into urban life initially via West Kingston, and there they join many of the urban misfits and social and economic failures. There they also find themselves among many striving people who are the unwitting victims of their national history and social and economic system. The area is commonly and correctly viewed as a national problem that has been aggravated by recent trends of change. The reader will recall that it

---

[4] Melvin M. Tumin and Arnold Feldman, *Social Class and Social Change in Puerto Rico*, Princeton, N. J.: Princeton University Press, 1961, p. 423.

was for these reasons that this area was chosen to be the issue focus of this research, and to provide the basis for the definition of the universe of leaders to be studied. Trench Town, the specific area sampled, is occupied largely by squatter-residents who command only meager resources with which to improve their life chances. A total of 132 interviews were completed with adults in a 25 per cent systematic random sample of households. (Further descriptions of the details of sampling and interviewing, and social characteristics of the sample are presented in Appendix 1).

Table 6. PERCENTAGE DISTRIBUTION OF JAMAICAN LEADERS AND URBAN LOWER-CLASS RESPONDENTS ACCORDING TO THEIR IMAGES OF THE FUTURE, EXPECTED EFFECTS OF INDEPENDENCE, AND EVALUATION OF PAST CHANGE

Item	Jamaican Leaders (Per Cent)	Urban Lower-Class Respondents (Per Cent)
Images of the future		
Favorable	61	49
About the same	4	24
Doubtful	35	27
Total	100	100
Number of cases	(54)	(130)
No answer	—	(2)
Expected effect of independence		
A favorable effect	38	32
No effect	48	21
Uncertain	6	38
An unfavorable effect	8	9
Total	100	100
Number of cases	(52)	(125)
No answer	(2)	(7)
Evaluation of past change		
Favorable	50	40
Unfavorable	50	60
Total	100	100
Number of cases	(54)	(116)
No answer	—	(16)

Comparison of the Jamaican leaders' images of the future with those held by the lower-class persons sampled in Kingston seems to support Tumin and Feldman's conclusion that persons in different social strata develop differing views of future possibilities.[5] These data, presented in Table 6, are comparisons of responses to two questions discussed earlier in addition to a third question regarding evaluations of Jamaica's recent

[5] *Ibid.*, p. 208, Table 12–6, and pp. 206–209.

history. The first comparison deals with the general images of Jamaica's future progress. The urban lower-class respondents were less likely to have favorable expectations for the nation's future than were the leaders. Forty-nine per cent of the West Kingston sample anticipated future progress for the people of Jamaica, whereas 61 per cent of the leaders held this view. About one quarter of the lower-class sample indicated that they expected things to be about the same in the future. Only four per cent of the leaders fell in this category.

It has probably been true in many new nations as it was in Jamaica, that one of the popular stereotypical conceptions which circulated just prior to independence was that the lower classes viewed the coming of independence as a panacea; that severance of ties with Britain would somehow free Jamaica to help poor Jamaicans. This notion is seriously questioned by the findings presented in Table 6. When asked about the effects of independence upon the future of Jamaica, the lower-class respondents indicated a great deal of uncertainty of expectations, or said that they expected no effects of any significance to flow from independence. Among the lower-class persons, 38 per cent were uncertain about the effects of independence, and an additional 21 per cent anticipated no effect. By comparison, 6 per cent of the leaders were uncertain about the impact of independence, and nearly half expected independence to have no effect on the nation's future. Both the leaders and the lower-class respondents infrequently predicted negative consequences from the achievement of independence. Favorable effects of independence were expected by 32 per cent of the lower-class respondents and 38 per cent of the leaders interviewed. It appears that the major difference between the leaders and the lower-class people regarding the expected effects of independence is the greater degree of uncertainty expressed by the urban lower-class persons. Certainly, from these data it does not appear to be the case that most of the urban lower classes expected political independence to transform Jamaica into a land of milk and honey. A total of 68 per cent of these people did not expect favorable consequences from nationhood, but rather they were uncertain about the outcome, or predicted no effect and even negative consequences.

The last question given in Table 6 has been mentioned only briefly before. The leaders and the lower-class respondents were asked, "Considering all the people of Jamaica, from 1938 to the present, in what year do you think they were best off — in 1938, today, or some year in between?" Those who said the present was better in all ways than earlier years were said to hold a favorable view of past change. The choice of a time in the past as better than the present was interpreted as an unfavorable perception of the major trend of change since 1938.

The leaders were found to be evenly divided on their evaluations of past change. Half indicated that the present was generally better than the past and that Jamaica's recent history had involved progressive trends. The West Kingston people were less likely to accept this evaluation of the recent history of their nation. Sixty per cent of the lower-class sample indicated that the present was not a high point in the trends of change, that the people of Jamaica were generally better off at some point in the recent past. Recalling our earlier discussion of the change in Jamaica in the last quarter-century, it may be somewhat surprising that a greater proportion of the lower-class respondents did not evaluate these changes more favorably. More detailed data for the lower-class persons, not presented in Table 6, showed that 12 per cent said that there was no time when the people of Jamaica were well off, and 1938 and today were equally hard times. Another 29 per cent, paying no heed to the advances that had been achieved, said that 1938 was better than the present. I think that these findings must be viewed as a rejection by lower-class respondents of the suggestion that they have in any way been included in Jamaica's development. Moreover, these findings lend credence to those critics of Jamaica's development program who have been pointing to an increasing maldistribution of income, goods, and services. Broadly speaking, the data in Table 6 affirm the idea that people from different social strata are likely to hold somewhat differing views of their nation, its history, and its potential. The Jamaican leaders studied here were more favorably impressed with political, economic, and social trends in Jamaica than were lower-class persons, and leaders were also more likely to predict progressive development of their nation's potential than were lower-class respondents.

CROSS-NATIONAL COMPARISONS

The interpretation and significance of these data on Jamaicans' views of their nation's past and future progress may be augmented by reference to comparable material from other nations. Cross-national comparisons can provide a frame of reference that will help establish a standard of evaluation. Without such comparisons it would be difficult to determine whether the findings reported here should be considered relatively alarming or reassuring. Unfortunately, because of variations in samples, methods, and purposes of data collection, not all of the comparisons to be made here are as reliable as one would like, but they are still relevant and worthwhile. The data for comparison, summarized in Table 7, include findings from studies conducted in Puerto Rico, India, United States, Cuba, Panama, Dominican Republic, Brazil, and Nigeria.

Melvin M. Tumin and Arnold Feldman in their research on social class and social change in Puerto Rico offer some points of comparison

Table 7. INTERNATIONAL COMPARISONS OF PAST, PRESENT, FUTURE EVALUATIONS

Country and Sample	Date of Study	Present Better than Past (Per Cent)	No. of Cases on Which the Per Cent is Based	Favorable Future (Per Cent)	No. of Cases on Which the Per Cent is Based
Jamaican leaders	(1962)	50	(54)	61	(54)
Jamaican lower class	(1962)	40	(114)	49	(130)
Puerto Ricans (total sample)a	(1954)	81	(979)	62	(996)
Highly educated group (9 years or more)		84	(235)	61	(241)
No education		76	(237)	51	(238)
Indian Parliamentariansb	(1958)	75	(103)	75	(103)
United Statesc	(1959)	39	(2534)	53	(2399)
Cuba	(1960)	89	(1445)	75	(1445)
Panama	(1962)	71	(1283)	80	(1243)
Dominican Republic	(1962)	58	(2344)	95	(2320)
Brazil	(1960–61)	48	(1808)	81	(1452)
Nigeria	(1962–63)	90	(2416)	93	(2042)

a Melvin Tumin with Arnold Feldman, *Social Class and Social Change in Puerto Rico*, Princeton, N.J.: Princeton University Press, 1961, p. 202, Table 12–1; and p. 208, Table 12–6; some percentages were recomputed by this writer.

b Lloyd A. Free, *Six Allies and a Neutral*, Glencoe, Ill.: The Free Press, 1959, p. 14.

c The data for the U.S., Cuba, Panama, Dominican Republic, Brazil, and Nigeria are from Hadley Cantril, *The Pattern of Human Concerns*, New Brunswick, N.J.: Rutgers University Press, 1965. The figures presented here were recomputed excluding the non-respondents. This was necessary to make the desired cross-national comparisons because of the widely varying proportions of non-respondents that were included in the original percentages reported by Cantril. The number of cases on which the percentages are based refers to card units in weighted samples, less the non-respondents. Thus, these figures are percentages of cases in which national ratings on a 10 point ladder-scale shifted upward from past to present, and from present to future.

with these Jamaican findings. They say, "Those who have received less of the good things in life ought to sum up differently their expectations and their views of social trends." Proceeding from this proposition, they asked Puerto Rican people to compare life today with that of the past.[6] Their tabulations (Table 7) reveal that 81 per cent of their total sample, and more than 75 per cent at each class (educational) level, thought life today was better than in past years. The more relevant comparisons of the Jamaican and Puerto Rican findings are based on the subgroups of Puerto Ricans most similar to the two Jamaican

---

[6] The question asked in Puerto Rico was, "How do you feel about life today for young people who are just starting out, compared to what it was like when you started out? Considering everything, is life today better, the same, or worse than when you started out?" Tumin and Feldman, *op. cit.*, p. 202.

groups. Specifically, the two highest groups of Puerto Ricans by level of education attained, nine to twelve years, and thirteen or more, when combined are most comparable to the Jamaican leaders. At the other extreme, the group with no education will be compared with the Jamaican urban lower-class sample.

Today was thought better than earlier years by 84 per cent of the educated Puerto Ricans, compared to 76 per cent of the group without the benefit of education. Half of the Jamaican leaders thought the present was better than the past, while 40 per cent of the lower-class Jamaicans stated this view. These variations by social level within each national group are consistent with Tumin and Feldman's conclusion that, ". . . the higher the class, the higher the per cent who say that life is better today than earlier and the fewer who say that life is worse, with small differences among classes."[7] But both Jamaican groups were considerably less likely to hold this view than were Puerto Ricans. The reasons for this difference may be found in the world renowned success of the Puerto Rican development program in recent years.

Concerning the future, Tumin and Feldman found the general population of Puerto Rico to have quite favorable expectations, with more than half at all class levels indicating the belief that the future would be better.[8] When the subgroups of the Puerto Rican and Jamaican samples are compared there is very little difference. In fact, for the educated group of Puerto Ricans, and the Jamaican leaders there was no difference, with 61 per cent of both groups seeing a more favorable future.[9] Comparisons of the less educated Puerto Ricans with the lower-class Jamaicans showed that the two groups were practically identical in their expectations of future progress. Fifty-one per cent of the Puerto Ricans, and 49 per cent of the Jamaican lower-class group saw the future to be better than the present.

Another comparison is possible with these data; that is, the trend of change perceived by the two national groups. While 84 per cent of the educated Puerto Ricans thought today was better than the past, less — 61 per cent — thought the future would be better than the present. Similarly, 76 per cent of the lowest class level viewed the present as an improvement over the past, but only 51 per cent projected this line of improvement into the future. In this regard, Tumin and Feldman stated, "In brief, there is a growing tendency for people . . . either to be more dubious about how the future will be, compared to the present,

[7] *Ibid.*, p. 203.
[8] *Ibid.*, p. 208, Table 12–6.
[9] Percentage for Puerto Ricans computed by this writer from Table 12–6, *ibid.*, p. 208.

Norman Washington Manley, Q.C., former Premier of Jamaica and leader of the People's National Party. (*Courtesy of Jamaica Information Service*).

The late Sir Donald B. Sangster, K.C.V.O., who was Prime Minister for a few short weeks before his death had also served as Acting Prime Minister and as Minister of Finance. (*Courtesy of Jamaica Information Service*).

Members of the Jamaica Labour Party Cabinet after elections of 1962, with Sir Kenneth Blackburne, the Governor (front row, fourth from left). Front row from left to right they are: Hon. E. L. Allen, Education; Hon. R. C. Lightbourne, Trade and Industry; Hon. D. B. Sangster, Finance; Sir Alexander Bustamante, Kt., Premier; Hon. D. C. Tavares, Housing; Hon. K. A. N. Jones, Communications and Works; back row, left to right: Hon. R. A. McNeil, Home Affairs; Hon. H. L. Shearer, Minister without Portfolio; Hon. Wilton O. Hill, Minister without Portfolio; Hon. J. P. Gyles, Agriculture and Lands; Hon. N. N. Ashenheim, C. B. E., Minister without Portfolio; Hon. Dr. H. W. Eldemire, Health; Hon. E. P. G. Seaga, Development and Welfare; Hon. L. G. Newland, Labor. (*Courtesy of Government Public Relations Office*).

Independence Celebrations: Prime Minister reviews military band. *(Courtesy of Jamaica Tourist Board)*.

Independence Celebrations: watching a parade in downtown Kingston. *(Courtesy of Jamaica Information Service)*.

Independence Celebrations: Children representing their schools in a parade. (*Courtesy of Jamaica Information Service*).

Street scene in Kingston. (*Courtesy of Jamaica Information Service*).

People's National-Party National Workers' Union Labour Day Celebration. (*Gleaner Photo*).

Higglers bring produce to markets. (*Courtesy of Jamaica Information Service*).

A home in Trench Town. (*Photograph by Amador Packer*).

or to feel it will remain about the same."[10] The comparable figures for Jamaicans indicate a direct reversal of the findings for Puerto Rico. Half of the Jamaican leaders saw the present as better than the past, and 61 per cent expected further progress. Among the lower-class Jamaican sample, 40 per cent saw the present as better than the past, and 49 per cent expected the future to be better as well. These last comparisons show that while the general level of satisfaction with the present is lower in Jamaica than in Puerto Rico, there is among Jamaicans a greater frequency of belief in their nation's future potential than in its past progress. Among the Puerto Ricans this was not the case; at all class levels, they were more likely to evaluate past changes favorably than to anticipate a favorable future.[11] These differences between the two island societies may accurately reflect differences in past achievements and unrealized potential. But, this should not be allowed to obscure the fact that relatively fewer Jamaicans than Puerto Ricans favorably evaluated past change while no more Jamaicans than Puerto Ricans had favorable images of the future.

A survey conducted in India of a cross-section of the Lok Sabha, the Indian Parliament, allows another comparison with Jamaica. Lloyd A. Free reported that the dominant attitude of Indian parliamentarians toward the future was one of "determined optimism."[12] Free assessed the Indians' view of past and future progress by means of a 10-point "ladder, or striving scale." His question specified the time referent as five years ago and five years hence. He found that, ". . . three-quarters of the parliamentarians indicated that they thought India was higher on the ladder than it had been five years ago, and an equal proportion said that it would be higher still five years from now."[13]

When compared to these Indian political elites, the Jamaican leaders (and the better educated strata of Puerto Ricans) fall short in their belief that the future will surpass the present. The Indians, like the Puerto Ricans, were a great deal higher than the Jamaican leaders in their sense of progress from past to present. These differences between India and Jamaica may stem from the fact that India is a slightly older nation whose development programs are coming to maturity, or the difference may more likely be a result of the clearly based political status of the Indian respondents. Variations in the anticipation of future progress by different types of leaders in Jamaica will be examined later.

---

[10] *Ibid.*, p. 209.
[11] *Ibid.*, p. 202, Table 12–1; and p. 208, Table 12–6.
[12] Lloyd A. Free, *Six Allies and a Neutral,* Glencoe, Ill.: The Free Press, 1959, p. 14.
[13] *Ibid.*

Additional comparisons of findings from Jamaica with those for the United States, Cuba, Panama, Dominican Republic, Brazil, and Nigeria are summarized in Table 7. These data are drawn from a series of studies conducted in several countries by Hadley Cantril and associates.[14] The figures for the United States allow comparisons of attitudes toward the trend of change expressed by a national sample in an advanced industrial nation, and provide some information concerning the relationship between levels of national development and the images of the past and future held by the people of the nation. The next four countries were chosen for comparison because they more or less surround Jamaica socially, economically, and geographically. The last nation included for comparison is Nigeria which like Jamaica is a former British colony that has recently become an independent nation. These countries are ranked in Table 7 according to their level of socioeconomic development as determined by Cantril by means of a composite index based on 11 indicators of development.[15]

In each of these six countries the respondents were asked to rate their nation on a 10-step "self-anchoring striving scale" indicating where they thought their nation stood five years ago, where it stands today, and where it will stand five years from now in relation to the best and worst possible national situations they can imagine. The figures presented in Table 7 for these six countries are the percentages of respondents who shifted their ratings of their nation upward on the 10 point ladder-scale. These respondents perceived their present national situation to be generally better than its past, and expected its future to be better than its present standing. It is unfortunately true that using only these percentages of persons who shifted their ratings omits a great deal of additional information reported by Cantril. For example, these figures do not indicate whether the initial ratings of the nation were very low or high, or whether the perceived change from past to future is little or great. That is, they do not show whether the respondents shifted their ratings upward by one, three, or five steps on the ladder-scale. Cantril reports this more detailed information by presenting the average ladder

[14] Hadley Cantril, *The Pattern of Human Concerns*, New Brunswick, N. J.: Rutgers University Press, 1965; Hadley Cantril and Lloyd A. Free, "Hopes and Fears for Self and Country," *The American Behavioral Scientist*, (supplement), IV (October, 1962); and Hadley Cantril, "A Study of Aspirations," *Scientific American*, 208 (February, 1963), pp. 3–8.

[15] This composite index of development includes indicators of general welfare, development of communications, industrialization, urbanization, and education. Some of the indicators are: Gross National Product per capita, number of doctors per 10,000 population, number of vehicles, telephones, and radios per 1,000 population, energy consumption, size of non-agricultural labor force, per cent of urban population, literacy, and others. See Cantril, *The Pattern of Human Concerns, op. cit.*, pp. 193–194.

ratings for the nation, and by indicating the average shifts up or down the ladder over time. These details are not included here because the Jamaican data do not allow such detailed comparisons, but some of these findings for the six countries will be summarized in order to augment the comparisons of percentages made in Table 7.

Generally, Cantril found that people in the more advanced nations rated their countries relatively low on the ladder-scale in relation to their ideals for the nation, and conversely, the people in all of the poorer, less developed countries, rated their nations relatively high. Moreover, he found that the less developed the country, the greater was the overall shift in average ladder ratings assigned by the people. So, for example, the largest shifts in national ratings were for those nations that were objectively low on his index of socio-economic development, and that had recently gained independence or experienced some revolutionary political changes. This is implicitly shown in Table 7 by the high percentages for Cuba, studied shortly after Castro's take-over; for Nigeria, recently independent; and for the Dominican Republic, surveyed soon after the assassination of President Raphael Trujillo. Brazil's history of economic and political instability, and the stirrings of development, are reflected in the fact that slightly less than half of the people rated the present as better than the past, but, as in all of the less developed countries studied by Cantril, the percentage of persons expecting a more favorable future was very high.

The revolutionary fervor, the exuberant spirit of independence, and the awakening to vast realms of new possibilities that characterize the developing countries does not have an apparent counterpart in the more advanced nations. The relatively low figures for the United States illustrate Cantril's generalization that the more advanced nations showed the smallest shift in national ratings over time. Even though it may be the case that the advanced nations are in fact experiencing more change than the less developed nations, these changes are not perceived and evaluated as favorably as the changes in the other nations. Concerning these findings for the United States, Cantril stated that the ". . . least relative progress was foreseen by Americans who rated their country high for the present and seemed to feel that it would continue a steady growth."[16] For the most part, the Americans expected continued but certainly not spectacular development toward the desired future of the nation.

The major direction of change experienced and expected in all of these countries, including Jamaica, is one of continued improvement. Except for the United States, a greater percentage of people in each

[16] *Ibid.*, p. 192.

nation expected a favorable future than did the Jamaicans interviewed, and the Jamaicans were also somewhat less likely to view their recent history as favorable than were Cantril's respondents. It is particularly true that the Jamaican lower-class respondents less frequently viewed Jamaica's past and possible future in favorable terms when compared to people from these other developing countries. In this connection, it must be remembered that Cantril's findings refer to national cross-sections of the populations, while the findings for Jamaica are based on extremes of lower-class persons in West Kingston on one hand, and national leaders on the other.

Despite the fact that the relevance of these comparisons is strained somewhat by the different nature of the studies and samples, the variation in attitudes toward past and future displayed in these six countries does call attention to the relationship between these attitudes and levels of national development, and should aid in assessing the findings for Jamaica. One question prompted by these comparisons for example, is why lower-class Jamaicans were apparently much less optimistic than Cubans, Panamanians, and citizens of the Dominican Republic, all nations that approximate Jamaica's level of development. Furthermore, in contrast to Jamaica, it was the poorest people in Cuba who held the most favorable expectations for the nation's future, while the more educated and politically experienced Cubans expressed more modest expectations.[17]

Following Cantril's lead, one explanation of these findings is that in these less developed countries where living conditions for the mass of the people are bad and change is overdue, any change that is interpreted as an improvement and taken to indicate that a favorable trend has begun raises the hopes and expectations for spectacular changes that are far out of proportion to the initial change.[18] Thus, Castro's successful action against the corrupt Batista government gave rise to soaring predictions by poorer Cubans in a little more than a year after the new revolutionary regime was established. And in Nigeria, the great fears expressed by most Nigerians concerning political instability and problems of tribal and regional loyalties were eased somewhat by the formation of the new nation for which more than 90 per cent anticipated a brighter future. These changes provided the impetus for the development of great expectations in these countries. But, perhaps for Jamaicans the advent of independence was not a sufficiently significant change to create widespread images of a favorable future for the nation. In fact, as mentioned in the earlier discussion of the findings in Table 6,

[17] *Ibid.*, p. 312.
[18] *Ibid.*, p. 305.

a majority of Jamaicans, both among the leaders and the lower-class people, did not expect significantly favorable consequences to flow from independence, and this is reflected in their less frequent expressions of favorable future expectations for their nation than were found by Cantril for Nigeria and those countries that recently experienced revolutionary change. It is also possible, however, that some of the uncertainty and skepticism among Jamaicans about the outcome of independence was because the interviewing for this study was done just prior to independence rather than two years after as was the case for the Nigerian study. The Jamaicans were stating their expectations concerning the effects of independent status, and they had not yet had the opportunity to witness and evaluate the effects of the change.

A final comparison of Jamaicans' views of the future may be made with the attitudes toward the future held by Mexican peasant farmers. These data were reported by Mirin and Stinchcombe as part of a study of political mobilization of peasants in the state of Aguascalientes. The peasants were asked: "Do you think future years will be better than, worse than, or the same as past years?" Half of their 119 respondents refused to answer, often indicating that "Only God knows." Of those who answered, 72 per cent thought that the future would be better than the past.[19] If we assume that the "no answer" split in the same way, we find the Jamaicans, both leaders and lower classes, have less faith in the future than those in yet other social and cultural setting. Thus, in essentially every comparison we have seen, the Jamaicans studied fall short in the favorableness of their views of their nation's future. Unfortunately, these comparisons can be made only for the most general question concerning the nation's future, and because of the many differences between the various studies, the explanations offered about the differences in findings can only be partial and tentative.

In this chapter we have examined the images of the future of Jamaica that were expressed by a segment of the national leadership and by members of the urban lower classes. Among the leaders, the majority generally were optimistic about the future of their nation, though most of them did not expect improvements to come from the achievement of independence. Independence was viewed by many of the leaders as one in a series of important steps in the development of the nation-state, and was not too significant in itself. On the more specific topic of the future of West Kingston and the problems of the urban

---

[19] Linda Mirin and Arthur L. Stinchcombe, "The Political Mobilization of Mexican Peasants," presented at the meetings of the American Sociological Association, Montreal, Canada, September, 1964.

lower classes, certainly one of the major trials facing the nation, the leaders were more uncertain and doubtful than optimistic. And, the lower-class persons from the area of West Kingston were also less sanguine about the future in all respects than the leaders were. Like the leaders, they also did not have great hopes for improvements resulting from independence itself.

The expectations of the leaders, both favorable and doubtful, were based largely on their ideas about the likelihood of maintaining a sufficiently high level of economic growth to meet the needs of the nation, and on the likelihood that the people of Jamaica would accept the social responsibilities and duties of citizenship necessary for the success of independence. Another frequently mentioned and related concern of the leaders was whether or not the island-society would be able to provide expanded opportunities for education, and be able to reduce the remaining social barriers to achievement and mobility. The leaders who were more confident about these problems and their solution were in the majority.

In comparing nations and the dominant images of the future that their people express, we can see that levels of development of the nation and the nature of the prevailing social and political organization are importantly related to the attitudes concerning change and the future. But, within a single nation the major questions that emerge as central to this study are why the Jamaicans studied, particularly the leaders, have such differing expectations for the future of their nation; and how it is that many of them can cite the same reasons for dire predictions as are given by others as the foundation for favorable images of the future. In the chapters that follow, some factors are offered to explain what differentiates the optimistic leaders from those who speak like prophets of gloom.

CHAPTER 4 An Index of Belief in Progress

In this chapter, the four questions used thus far as separate indicators of Jamaican leaders' images of the future are combined into a single Index of Belief in Progress. This index conveniently converts the leaders' images of Jamaica's future into a single score that will be used in the analyses carried out in later chapters. Although the unity of content of these questions has not been stressed, it has probably been evident to the reader. The essential similarity of these questions in their combination of both evaluative and temporal aspects and their reference to substantially one universe of attitudes suggest that they are unidimensional.

The hypothesis of unidimensionality is that these four questions about Jamaica's future are a sample of possible items drawn from a single universe of attitude content. This universe is belief or disbelief in progress. As measured here, belief in progress in Jamaica is the affirmation that the future will be better than the present; that the advent of independence will have beneficial consequences; that the future of Western Kingston and its people will be better than the present; and finally, that there is not likely to be a violent outbreak of civil disorder in Western Kingston. This is one extreme of the continuum. At the opposite end of the scale should be found those persons who negate these beliefs; those who expect a doubtful future, see an ineffective political change in independence, and anticipate misfortune and violence for the people of Western Kingston. The persons who believe in progress attach a positive value to the process and direction of the social, economic, and political changes they foresee. The Index of Belief in Progress is based on the leaders' evaluative statements about the direction of these changes, and is thought of as being about a process, rather than a finite end-state toward which that process may, or may not, be moving. Thus, those who believe in progress are not to be thought of as believing in the future achievement of a single perfect state, but simply that change will continue in a favorable or beneficial direction.

Labeling these beliefs "progress" is justified on two levels of reasoning. Most simply, avoiding for the moment the specific content of future expectations, this use of "progress" is no more than an equation of that concept with "betterment." Those who believe the future will be better than the present, believe in progress, and vice versa. This says nothing *a priori* about the nature of "betterment." It requires the leaders to supply the defining criteria of these evaluations.[1] But, in fact, the content of the view of progress held by Jamaican leaders was essentially consistent with the Western world's idea of progress coming out of the rationalism of the Enlightenment. The words of Edward Gibbon, said to be the greatest Enlightenment historian, convey the meaning of this idea of progress. He wrote, ". . . that every age of the world has increased, and still increases, the real wealth, the happiness, the knowledge, and perhaps the virtue, of the human race."[2] Thus, my use of the term "progress," following the historian, E. H. Carr, refers to the process of developing human potential for increased knowledge and understanding, and to the process of increasing material resources, which allow greater and greater control over ourselves and our social organization as well as our physical environment.[3]

SCALE ANALYSIS

The Index of Belief in Progress, defined by the four questions presented in the preceding chapter (Table 5), was tested for unidimensionality as a cumulative scale by means of a Guttman scale analysis, following the Cornell scaling technique.[4]

The final results of the application of scale analysis to the Index of

---

[1] Theoretically speaking, a reactionary who anticipated that Jamaica might have an authoritarian or dictatorial regime would be a believer in progress if he also defined that change in government as betterment for Jamaica. The scale used in this analysis did not have to account for any such cases however.

[2] Edward Gibbon, *The Decline and Fall of the Roman Empire*, ch. xxxviii, quoted in Edward Hallett Carr, *What is History*, New York: A. A. Knopf, 1962, p. 146.

[3] *Ibid.*, pp. 156–157; see also Bruce Mazlish, "The Idea of Progress," *Daedalus*, 92 (Summer, 1963), pp. 458–459; and Erville Bartlett Woods, "Progress as a Sociological Concept," *The American Journal of Sociology*, XII (May, 1907), pp. 810–814. Alternatively, this might also be conceptualized as increases in the basic capabilities of a nation to deal with the systemic problems of national integration, international accommodation, political participation, and welfare distribution as discussed by Gabriel Almond; see Gabriel Almond, "Political Systems and Political Change," *The American Behavioral Scientist*, VI (June, 1963), pp. 3–10.

[4] This method of scale analysis is extensively discussed in the following: Louis Guttman, "A Basis for Scaling Quantitative Data," *American Sociological Review*, IX (April, 1944), pp. 139–150; "The Cornell Technique for Scale and Intensity Analysis," *Educational and Psychological Measurements*, VII (Summer, 1947), pp. 247–280; and Chapters II and III in S. A. Stouffer, *et al.*, *Measurement and Prediction*, Princeton, N. J.: Princeton University Press, 1950, pp. 46–90.

Belief in Progress are summarized in Table 8. A coefficient of reproducibility of .894 was achieved, which is a satisfactory approximation to the criterion of .90 suggested by Guttman.[5] This coefficient of reproducibility shows sizeable improvement in prediction over the co-

Table 8. SCALE CRITERIA RELATED TO THE INDEX OF BELIEF IN PROGRESS

Scale Criteria	(N = 54)
1. Coefficient of reproducibility	.894
2. Range of marginal frequencies	The extreme modal categories contain 48 to 56 per cent of the responses. The remainder fall within that range. This range is sufficient to provide a range of scores.
3. Minimum marginal reproducibility	.545
4. Number of items and response categories	There are four items all of which are dichotomies.
5. Pattern of error	There is one segment of non-random error containing 6 responses.
6. Error-to-non-error ratio	No answer category has more error than non-error.

efficient of minimum marginal reproducibility of .545.[6] As might be concluded from the latter coefficient, the marginal frequencies in the modal response categories are in no case sufficiently extreme to result in spurious reproducibility.

Two factors warrant at least some skepticism concerning the undimensionality of the items defined as the Index of Belief in Progress. The first is the relatively small number of items in the index. Although Guttman has used as few as four to six statements,[7] he also has suggested that a small sample of items from a non-scalable universe might yield low error when all response categories are dichotomies. Secondly, examination of the scalogram reveals one segment of non-random error containing six responses. Although these errors constitute only 2 per cent of the total responses, they suggest the possibility of an additional variable in the index.[8] With these cautions in mind, the hypothesis of unidimensionality for the Index of Belief in Progress is tentatively accepted. These details of the index in relation to the criteria of scalability are shown in Table 8.

[5] Guttman, in Stouffer, *et al.*, *ibid.*, p. 89.
[6] Allen Edwards, *Techniques of Attitude Scale Construction*, New York: Appleton-Century-Crofts, Inc., 1957, pp. 191–193.
[7] *Ibid.*, p. 177.
[8] *Ibid.*, p. 196.

The percentage distribution of scale scores for the Jamaican leaders on the Index of Belief in Progress is shown in Table 9. This final distribution was arbitrarily dichotomized as close to the median as

Table 9. PERCENTAGE DISTRIBUTION OF JAMAICAN LEADERS ACCORDING TO SCALE SCORES ON THE INDEX OF BELIEF IN PROGRESS

Scale Score	Jamaican Leaders (Per Cent)
4 (Highest)	16.7
3	22.2
2	16.7
1	16.7
0 (Lowest)	27.7
Total	100.0
Number of cases	(54)
As dichotomized:	
2–4 (Believes in progress)	56
0–1 (Does not believe in progress)	44
Total	100
Number of cases	(54)

possible for purposes of later subgroup comparisons and analyses. Those leaders who gave favorable responses to at least two of the four items, and who received a scale score of two or more, were labeled as believing in progress. Those persons who scored zero or one, by giving unfavorable answers to at least three questions, were designated as persons who did not believe in progress. In this manner, 56 per cent of the Jamaican leaders were classified as believing in progress, and 44 per cent as not accepting this view. Although it would have been preferable to retain a larger number of categories, the small number of leaders interviewed required this dichotomous treatment.

Before proceeding to the question, "Who are the leaders who believe in progress?" let us turn back for a moment to the leaders' evaluations of past changes in Jamaica. It was shown in the preceding chapter (Table 6) that these Jamaican leaders were divided half-and-half on the endorsement of Jamaica's recent history. What of the relationship between these attitudes toward the past and the belief in progress? Concerning the interdependence between past change and future progress, E. H. Carr remarked that, "The belief that we have come from somewhere is closely linked with the belief that we are going somewhere."[9] The relevance of this conclusion may be seen by looking at Table 10. We see that two thirds of the leaders who believed in the

[9] Carr, op. cit., p. 176.

Table 10. PERCENTAGE OF JAMAICAN LEADERS WHO FAVORABLY EVALUATED PAST CHANGE BY BELIEF IN PROGRESS

Index of Belief in Progress	Percentage Who Favorably Evaluated Past Change	No. of Cases on Which the Per Cent is Based
Believes in progress	67	(30)
Does not believe in progress	29	(24)

future progress of Jamaica also favorably evaluated the changes which have taken place since 1938. Less than a third of those who did not affirm Jamaica's potential for progress perceived past change in a favorable light. The sizeable percentage difference which separates these two groups of leaders underscores Carr's further conclusion that interests in the past and future are interconnected because the past and future are indeed part of one time-span.[10]

While the implications of this interaction between evaluations of past and future change are many, it clearly supports the conception of the Index of Belief in Progress. The index, while based on evaluations of the future, is here shown to be also linked to interpretations of past change. This allows added confidence to be placed in the validity of the designation "belief in progress," since the major trend of these past changes can also be interpreted as progressive. As noted above, one of the major phenomena of Jamaican social history has been the trend toward equality and the increasing internal inclusiveness of Jamaican society.[11] Many of the leaders with whom we are here concerned had a part in leading these changes, and the personal lives of still more were affected by those trends.[12] The leader's evaluations of these trends, and their belief in progress, may, as a result, be thought of as part of a larger ideological commitment affecting their attitudes toward their changing society. This possibility will be discussed again in the analyses of the belief in progress.

SOCIAL DIFFERENTIATION AND BELIEF IN PROGRESS

The impact of variations in belief in progress upon the process and direction of future change is conditioned partially by the various social

---

[10] Carr, *op. cit.*, p. 142.

[11] See Chapter 2, *supra;* and Wendell Bell, "Equality and Attitudes of Elites in Jamaica," *Social and Economic Studies,* XI (December, 1962), pp. 409–432; see also his *Jamaican Leaders,* Chapter 2.

[12] The changing composition of the Jamaican legislature in recent years is only one of the more visible signs of this fact.

positions held by the leaders studied, and by their social characteristics. In other words, the answer to the question, "Who are the leaders who believe in progress in Jamaica?", is partly a structural one. Certainly, in the Jamaica of today, some social characteristics and positions are more highly valued than others, and, consequently, some of these persons may be more crucial in the determination of future outcomes. Answers to the "Who?" question concerning the variation in belief in progress will also provide the necessary background to deal with the "Why?" of variations in belief in progress.

Because the belief in progress may have been affected by the general elections of April, 1962, and by the repudiation of the Peoples' National Party (PNP) government, it is important that we examine the relationship between the leaders' belief in progress and their political party preference.

In this case, it was desirable not only to determine the effect of party preference *per se* upon the belief in progress, but also to delineate, as far as possible, the effects of the election and the resulting change in government. For this reason, those leaders who preferred the PNP should be considered separately from all others, including those who preferred the JLP and those for whom there was no indication of party preference. Looking at the top of Table 11, we can observe that the leaders who preferred the PNP were less likely to believe in progress than those with other political preferences. I have no doubt that a large part of this difference must be explained by reference to the outcome of the elections, which undoubtedly crushed some of the idealism and confidence with which the PNP viewed the future of Jamaica. Those leaders who were not adherents of the PNP, and who had probably lost nothing, but rather gained by the election outcome, were considerably more likely to believe in progress than were PNP adherents.

The variations in belief in progress by selected social characteristics which are summarized here are presented in detail in Table 11. In addition to political party preference, the clearest differences that emerge are by race-color, occupational rating,[13] and religious preference. Those who are brown in skin color, have a high occupational rating, and are members of the Anglican Church, were most likely to believe in progress. When political party preference is controlled, each

[13] The measure of occupational ratings was adapted by Wendell Bell for use in Jamaica from W. Lloyd Warner, Marchia Meeker, and Kenneth Eells, *Social Class in America*, Chicago: Science Research Associates, Inc., 1949, pp. 140–141; and Carson McGuire, "Social Status, Peer Status, and Social Mobility," a mimeographed memorandum for research workers based upon procedures used in studies for the Committee on Human Development, University of Chicago, Chicago, Ill., 1948.

Table 11. PERCENTAGE OF JAMAICAN LEADERS WHO BELIEVE IN PROGRESS BY SELECTED SOCIAL CHARACTERISTICS

Selected Characteristic	Percentage Who Believe In Progress	No. of Cases on which the Per Cent is Based
Political Party Preference		
Jamaica Labour Party	69	(13)
Peoples' National Party	42	(26)
Other	67	(15)
Age		
50 and over	55	(20)
40–49	50	(22)
39 and under	67	(12)
Education		
University or college graduate	59	(17)
Some university or college	56	(9)
Secondary school or less	54	(28)
Race-Color		
White	50	(14)
Brown	79	(14)
Black	46	(26)
Occupational Rating		
1 (Highest)	68	(28)
2–4 (Lowest)	42	(26)
Religious Preference		
Anglican	80	(15)
Other Protestant	56	(16)
Roman Catholic	57	(7)
Jewish	—	(1)

of these groups remains highest on belief in progress.[14] Those leaders who were under 40 years of age were somewhat more likely to believe in progress than either of the older groups, however this held true only for the adherents of the PNP. Among the JLP and others, differences in age had little or no effect on belief in progress. Moreover, among the university-educated leaders this relationship between age and belief in progress was reversed with the older leaders more likely to report a favorable future for the island than the younger respondents. Taken alone, educational attainment was only slightly related to belief in progress, with the highest educated leaders being most likely to affirm Jamaica's potential for progress. This relationship with education was considerably stronger among the oldest and intermediate age groups and for those leaders who preferred the PNP. It reversed in the cases

---

[14] The use of the word "control" in this research in reference to partial relationships involving dichotomized variables should be interpreted as an approximation to more exact elimination of variation due to third variables.

of the leaders who were not adherents of the PNP and among those under 40 years of age.

Additional information about differences in belief in progress is presented in Table 12. The percentage of Jamaican leaders who be-

Table 12. PERCENTAGE OF JAMAICAN LEADERS WHO BELIEVE IN PROGRESS BY TYPE OF ELITE POSITION

Type of Elite Position	Percentage Who Believe In Progress		No. of Cases on which the Per Cent is Based	
Politicians		57		(21)
Members of Parliament	69		(13)	
Parish Councillors	38		(8)	
Government Officers		38		(16)
Civil Servants	40		(10)	
Jamaica Social Welfare Commission	33		(6)	
Non-Governmental Community Welfare Leaders		71		(17)
Clergy	78		(9)	
Other	63		(8)	

lieved in progress is shown by the type of elite position they held.[15] By far the group most strongly committed to belief in progress was the non-governmental community welfare leaders. More persons of this group, made up of religious leaders and leaders of voluntary welfare associations such as YMCA, YWCA, and youth clubs, were likely to believe in progress than any other single subgroup. The members of the clergy led this group, with 78 per cent believing in progress, suggesting again that attitudes toward progress may be some function of broader ideological commitments.

The elected politicians were next highest in belief in progress with 57 per cent; but there was an important variation within that category. As shown in Table 12, those leaders who were members of the Kingston-St. Andrew Corporation (KSAC), the municipal governing body, were not likely to believe in progress. This finding becomes less surprising when it is realized that the local government of Kingston was dominated by PNP councillors until the KSAC was dissolved in 1964 under the JLP regime, and when it is recalled that PNP adherents were generally less likely to believe in progress. It is also possible that their

---

[15] The leaders holding more than one elite position were classified by that position which was most relevant to their role in dealing with the urban lower classes and Western Kingston.

close association with the inefficiencies and alleged corruption of Kingston local government was enough to destroy any man's faith in the possibility of a favorable future. Among the elected politicians at the national level, about two thirds of the Members of Parliament who were interviewed indicated a belief in progress. While two of these were PNP representatives, the remainder were Government Members including many Cabinet Ministers. This finding for Members of Parliament is similar to that for the Indian legislators reported by Free.[16]

The members of the government service, including civil servants and the Jamaica Social Welfare Commission staff, were not strongly convinced of Jamaica's future progress. The lowest figure in the table is found opposite the Welfare Commission. It is probable that this finding may also be explained by reference to the political party preferences of the respondents. On the whole, the Members of Parliament, and the non-governmental leaders were most likely to believe in progress, and the Parish Councillors and Government Officers were least likely to hold this positive outlook.

In this chapter, a cumulative scale, the Index of Belief in Progress, was constructed, and its unidimensionality was tested by the Guttman scaling technique. The index was accepted as a unitary scale for the measurement of belief in progress in Jamaica. Also, it was shown empirically that the favorable evaluation of past change was clearly related to belief in the progressive nature of future change. Finally, the distribution of belief in progress was specified by the introduction of selected social characteristics of the leaders, and by the type of elite positions they held.

The task has been set for the analysis which remains, namely, to provide answers to the question: "Why do some of these leaders believe in progress and others not?" One might ask, "After all, don't they all live in the same Jamaica?" They are all leaders of one sort or another whose duties and responsibilities are relevant to the urban lower class. They ought to know what's going on, and what planned changes are in the works. What explains the differences in their views of the future, and their belief in the progress of the new nation? These questions are taken up in succeeding chapters.

[16] Lloyd A. Free, *Six Allies and a Neutral*, Glencoe, Ill.: The Free Press, 1959, p. 14.

CHAPTER 5   Equality and Belief in Progress

Belief in progress is an idea by which man may interpret his condition, past and present, and by which he may justify his actions regarding his future. As an ideological commitment, belief in progress has served, since the Enlightenment, as an interpretation of life, and a reason for living. Yet, it is only one of the views and values to which men may be committed. Another is the principle giving rise to the criteria of worthiness of our fellow man to share the rights and responsibilities of that progress. I refer specifically to the idea of equality.

The idea of equality and the idea of progress have a logical similarity: both are what may be called normative ideas, or ideals. As suggested by Talcott Parsons, the referent of a normative idea may or may not actually exist. If it does exist, the normative idea implies the obligation to protect or maintain its existence. If it does not exist, the normative implication is ". . . an obligation to attempt its realization at some future time."[1] Both the belief in equality and belief in progress are ideas with this normative or obligatory quality. It is in this sense that I shall speak of the ideal of equality and the ideal of progress.

The Age of Enlightenment, and particularly the French revolutionary movement in the second quarter of the nineteenth century, saw the close association of the ideals of equality and progress.[2] For the most part the writings of Fontenelle and Voltaire made only small reference to the masses concerning progress, and saw the benefits of progress accruing to a privileged minority, but in the writings of Leroux, Condorcet, and especially Rousseau belief in progress was clearly associated with notions of social equality. For Rousseau and Condorcet, equality became the goal of social and political progress; for Leroux the approach to the egalitarian idea became the measure of progress, and the

[1] Talcott Parsons, "The Role of Ideas in Social Action," in his *Essays in Sociological Theory*, (rev. ed.), Glencoe: The Free Press, 1954, p. 21.
[2] This discussion is based primarily on the work of Professor J. B. Bury, *The Idea of Progress*, New York: Dover Publications, Inc., 1955.

goal would be achieved when man became synonymous with equal.³ This compatibility between belief in progress and the ideal of equality found in the history of modern thought underscores the relevance of egalitarianism to the focus of this research.

One of the vital forces in the drive for self-government and eventually for the attainment of political independence in Jamaica and elsewhere in the British Caribbean has been the ideology of equality. Our earlier discussion of the emergence of new leaders in the late 1930's and the rise of mass-based political parties and labor unions made it clear that the goals of many of these leaders and their organizations, particularly the early People's National Party, prominently included overcoming the striking inequalities of colonial Jamaican society. In their view this was to be done by achieving self-government and universal adult suffrage, and by using these political accomplishments to promote changes in the economy and society that would lessen inequality and favor more and more Jamaicans of all social levels.

Recent research by Charles C. Moskos, Jr., and additional findings reported by Moskos and Bell have demonstrated that in the colonial setting of the British Caribbean territories, egalitarian attitudes have been clearly associated with the desire for political independence.⁴ They state that "It is now clear that a key element in the images of the future that are shaping the new nations is to be found in the attitudes toward equality held by different elite groups." They conclude that "... attitudes toward equality constitute an important part of the ideology that has given rise to nationalist movements, and they also significantly influence the value premises of decision-making after the nationalist leaders come to power."⁵ Their conclusions strongly emphasize the important role of the ideal of equality in the images of the future held by new national leaders. In this chapter we shall see to what extent the images of the future of the Jamaican leaders, specifically their belief in progress, were associated with their acceptance of the imperatives of the ideology of equality.

THE MEASURE OF EGALITARIANISM

Social exclusion, the existence of barriers to full participation in society, is founded on the criteria of social worth that prevail in a society.

---

³ *Ibid.*, pp. 182–183; pp. 212–213; and p. 319.
⁴ Charles C. Moskos, Jr., *The Sociology of Political Independence: A Study of Nationalist Attitudes Among West Indian Leaders,* Cambridge, Mass.: Schenkman Publishing Co., 1967; and Charles C. Moskos, Jr., and Wendell Bell, "Political Attitudes in New Nations: Examples from the British Caribbean," in Carolyn W. Sherif and Muzafer Sherif (eds.), *Attitudes, Ego-Involvement, and Change,* New York: John Wiley & Sons, 1967, pp. 271–296.
⁵ Moskos and Bell, *op. cit.,* p. 272.

If worthiness is defined by characteristics that are ascribed rather than achieved, or if opportunities for achievement are differentially distributed according to an ascriptive system, incomplete social equality obtains. Basically, differential opportunity begets differential opportunities. Thus, social divisions based on inequity become both cause and consequence of the perpetuation of inequity. Although social differentiation need not imply inequality, the existence of a social hierarchy that restricts the internal inclusiveness of a society by the maintenance of ascriptive barriers to participation and achievement is inimical to the attainment of social equality. It is from this capsule of theory that the measure of egalitarianism was derived. Attitudes toward equality are here equated with attitudes toward the maintenance or reduction of status differences and ascriptive barriers which limit participation in the social process.

The Jamaican leaders were asked:

> Do you think it is advisable that any barriers to full interaction of people in Jamaica should be broken down, or are there some status differences which you feel should be maintained?

Those leaders who favored the reduction of such barriers to participation were categorized as egalitarian. Leaders who did not clearly favor the reduction of these limitations, or who gave equivocal answers were classified as inegalitarian. Two respondents who said there were no significant barriers were also classified as inegalitarian, since informed judgments agree that in fact there are barriers.

The percentage distribution of Jamaican leaders who were egalitarian and inegalitarian is shown in Table 13. Sixty per cent were found to be

Table 13. PERCENTAGE OF JAMAICAN LEADERS WHO ARE EGALITARIANS

Attitudes Toward Equality	Per Cent	No. of Cases
Egalitarian	60	(31)
Inegalitarian	40	(21)
Total	100	(52)

egalitarian. The remainder were not. There were insufficient data to classify two of the respondents properly.

The overall level of egalitarianism found among these leaders is fairly consistent with that found in previous studies of attitudes toward equality in Jamaica, even though different indices were used. In 1961, Moskos interviewed 24 Jamaican leaders for his study of nationalist attitudes among West Indian leaders, and he included a question designed to tap the leaders' attitudes toward equality. Specifically, he asked the leaders what they considered to be the essence of democracy, and classified as egalitarians those leaders who included in their answers such notions as equality of opportunity, classless society, social equality, or other similar features. On this basis, Moskos reports that half of the Jamaican leaders he interviewed were egalitarians.[6]

Bell completed a questionnaire study of Jamaican elites in 1958, that included an analysis of the distribution of egalitarian attitudes, using a seven-item cumulative scale adapted from the work of Seeman and others.[7] By dichotomizing the distribution of scale types as close to the median as possible, Bell designated 54 per cent of his sample of 231 Jamaican elites as egalitarian. In this fashion, Bell's respondents were required to give an egalitarian response to five of the seven items in order to be classified as egalitarian. Had the respondents been required only to give an egalitarian response to four of the seven items in order to be designated as egalitarians, the percentage of egalitarians would have increased from 54 to 72 per cent.

A study of 216 university students and 2,008 secondary school students in Jamaica in the spring of 1961, by James T. Duke, focused on the future of egalitarian ideals. Using the same measure of egalitarianism as Bell in his study of Jamaican elites, Duke found that this younger segment of the population of Jamaica also had quite favorable attitudes toward equality. These attitudes were found to be clearly related to educational level. Specifically, 46 per cent of the fifth form students, 59 per cent of the sixth form, and 76 per cent of the University students held egalitarian attitudes.[8]

These comparisons would seem to indicate that the findings reported here are consistent enough to warrant some confidence in their reliability. But, it should be noted that the measure used by both Bell and Duke was not exactly the same as the Index of Egalitarianism used here. The seven-item cumulative scale which they used focused on questions of social and economic rights, and problems of ascription versus achieve-

[6] *Ibid.*, p. 276.
[7] Wendell Bell, "Equality and Attitudes of Elites in Jamaica," *Social and Economic Studies*, XI (December, 1962), pp. 409–432. For a methodological discussion of the Index of Egalitarianism used in 1958 by Bell and later by Duke, see James A. Mau, "Scale Analyses of Status Perceptions and Status Attitudes in Jamaica and the United States," M. A. Report, University of California, Los Angeles, 1960; and James A. Mau, Richard J. Hill, and Wendell Bell, "Scale Analyses of Status Perception and Status Attitude in Jamaica and the United States," *Pacific Sociological Review*, IV (Spring, 1961), pp. 33–40.
[8] James T. Duke, "Equalitarianism Among Emergent Elites in a New Nation," unpublished Ph.D. dissertation, University of California, Los Angeles, 1963. The percentages were computed from Table 30.

ment as criteria in social interaction, whereas the single open-ended question used here was less specific.[9]

Although the multiple item index employed by Bell and Duke may afford somewhat greater reliability, the open-ended approach allowed considerable elaboration of the initial answers. The leaders were asked to specify the barriers which they thought limited participation of people in Jamaica. Of the leaders who responded to this question, 88 per cent mentioned social and economic class differences while 40 per cent mentioned race or color. Both class and race or color were named by 37 per cent of the leaders. Only one person mentioned race without also mentioning socio-economic class differences. Education was mentioned separately by 21 per cent of the leaders as an important barrier, and political party preference was included by 12 per cent.

The single finding of most interest is that 51 per cent of the leaders named socio-economic class and did not include race or color as an important limitation of opportunity for full participation in Jamaican society. This finding clearly supports the contention that socio-economic class differences rather than racial differences are the primary causal factor in discrimination and inequality in Jamaica. Again, a comparison with Bell's findings is appropriate and gives additional support to this proposition. One item in his Index of Equalitarianism explicitly refers to the restriction of membership in social clubs on a racial basis. Eight of every ten elites in his sample rejected race as a criterion for inclusion or exclusion. None of the other items referred to race specifically, and in no other case did the elites so frequently choose the extremely egalitarian response.[10] These data suggest that race or color are in fact less important as *causes* of discrimination in Jamaica than the class cleavage.[11]

---

[9] The decision not to use the Index of Equalitarianism used by Bell and Duke was based primarily on the choice of an intensive interview rather than the questionnaire technique. The flexibility of a single question with conversational probes was more consistent with the nature of the interview and seemed more congenial to the leaders interviewed.

[10] Bell, *op. cit.*, pp. 419–420.

[11] The assertion that race or color are less important than socio-economic class as a cause of discrimination in Jamaica is not based solely on the leaders' pronouncements, or on my personal observations alone. Other data suggest this conclusion. For example, (see Chapter 2 above) data on color and occupation in the 1943 census show that 60 per cent of the managers and officials and 84 per cent of the professionals were classified as either brown or black. The trends of change since 1943 have probably resulted in an increase in these percentages. These figures are based on the *Eighth Census of Jamaica and Its Dependencies, 1943*, as adapted by James T. Duke, "Equalitarianism Among Emergent Elites in a New Nation," *op. cit.*

Another indication of the primacy of class bias rather than race or color alone as the reason for discriminatory behavior is the common observation in Jamaica that a person's color seems to become lighter as he or she moves up the socio-economic ladder.

This discussion bears on a popular controversy among educated Jamaicans, and on the "myth of racial harmony," a favorite of debunkers. For example, one person interviewed said, "This talk of multi-racial harmony is a myth that will probably be officially maintained by the government." Within a few weeks of that interview, a booklet was published by the Government Public Relations Office which stated, "Above all, in our society, racial integration is no longer an ideal hope: it has become a profound and enriching reality."[12] In this regard, M. G. Smith has written, "... local 'nationalism' has developed a convenient mythology of 'progress' according to which race differences are held to be irrelevant in personal relations."[13] Acknowledging the existence of such mythology, of the gap between the ideal and the real, Vera Rubin points to the social value of the ideal. "Essentially ... the ideology serves as a charter for national unity.... The function of the ideal is important in this case, to achieve the harmony ... and the national unification of various racial and ethnic groups."[14] It is in the context of this public ideology that the Jamaican leaders studied clearly indicated the belief that race or skin color were a less important barrier to social participation than other socio-economic considerations.

This is not to say that color-bias is non-existent, or that shade preferences are uncommon. On the contrary, skin color is an important symbol, in conjunction with others, of the deference a person is to be accorded.[15] The situation seems to be, as one commentator has said:

> It is true to say that Jamaica is virtually free from racial discrimination, but that the black masses are openly discriminated against. Emphasis is on the word masses not black. Discrimination, if it can be called that, is against the masses as a historically-determined economic and cultural class, not as a racial group.[16]

[12] *One People*, Kingston: The Government Public Relations Office, 1962, p. 42.
[13] M. G. Smith, "The Political Implications of Jamaican Social Structure," unpublished paper, p. 12.
[14] Vera Rubin, "Culture, Politics, and Race Relations," *Social and Economic Studies*, XI (December, 1962), p. 437; her discussion of non-racialism as an ideology is also relevant; see pp. 434–437.
[15] For a detailed discussion of the cultural differences correlated with social position see M. G. Smith, "The Plural Framework of Jamaican Society," *The British Journal of Sociology*, XII (September, 1961), pp. 249–262.
[16] Katrin Norris, *Jamaica: The Search for an Identity*, London: Oxford University Press for the Institute of Race Relations, 1962, p. 61.

SOCIAL DIFFERENTIATION AND EGALITARIANISM

The percentage of leaders who were egalitarian is shown in Table 14 by selected social characteristics. Although few of the differences are large, most of them are in the direction we should expect from previous

Table 14. PERCENTAGE OF JAMAICAN LEADERS WHO ARE EGALITARIANS BY SELECTED SOCIAL CHARACTERISTICS

Selected Characteristic	Egalitarians (Per Cent)	No. of Cases on Which the Per Cent is Based
Political Party Preference		
Jamaica Labour Party	58	(12)
Peoples' National Party	69	(26)
Other	43	(14)
Age		
50 and over	58	(19)
40–49	59	(22)
39 and under	64	(11)
Education		
University or college graduate	60	(15)
Some university or college	67	(9)
Secondary school or less	57	(28)
Race–color		
White	54	(13)
Brown	54	(13)
Black	65	(26)
Occupational Rating		
1 (Highest)	50	(26)
2–4 (Lowest)	69	(26)
Religious Preference		
Anglican	67	(15)
Other Protestant	63	(16)
Roman Catholic	33	(6)
Jewish	—	(1)

research on egalitarianism in Jamaica. Also, almost every one of these correlations was in some manner complicated by political party preference of the leaders. Those leaders who preferred the Peoples' National Party (PNP) were most likely to have egalitarian attitudes, and those for whom no party preference was clear were least egalitarian, with the Jamaica Labour Party (JLP) adherents in an intermediate position.

Turning to the other social characteristics presented in Table 14, we see first that the younger leaders were more likely to hold favorable attitudes toward equality than the older groups. These differences were slight, but consistent with Bell's findings for a somewhat different type of Jamaican elite sample and with findings reported by Moskos and Bell for leaders in six British West Indian territories.[17] As they suggest, this finding may be explained by the increasing conservatism of increasing age, or by the fact that the new, younger leaders are the products of a social milieu that includes more favorable attitudes toward equality. It was also found here that among the Jamaican leaders the differences in egalitarianism by age were magnified for the PNP, but for the JLP and other preferences, age made no difference in attitudes toward equality.

The variation in egalitarianism by educational attainment, though not monotonic, showed that increased education is likely to promote egalitarian attitudes. This finding is consistent with those of Bell and Duke, though this correlation is lower.[18] Again, controlling for party preference, the original relationship is modified. Among the PNP there was no difference between the most and least educated, and those with some college or university were less likely to be egalitarians. Those leaders who were JLP and other with at least some university training were considerably more likely to have favorable attitudes toward equality than those with only secondary or training school education.

Those leaders who were white or brown in skin color were less often egalitarian than those of the darkest color. Fifty-four per cent of those classified as white or brown and almost two thirds of the black leaders held favorable attitudes to the promotion of equality. This is also consistent with the findings reported by Moskos and Bell.[19] Three quarters of both white and black who preferred the PNP were egalitarian, compared to half of the brown leaders. Among the white JLP and other, 44 per cent were egalitarian compared to 57 and 50 per cent of the brown and black groups.

Leaders who had low rather than high occupational ratings were more often egalitarian. Although this difference was considerably larger among the PNP, there was a small and contradictory effect of occupation among the JLP and other. Some of these findings may be due to the lack of variation in occupational rating among these leaders. The highest level of occupations contained about 50 per cent of the leaders, while the remainder were found distributed over three levels,

---

[17] Bell, *op. cit.*, p. 425; and Moskos and Bell, *op. cit.*, p. 278.
[18] These findings are also consistent with the conclusions of Adorno, *et al.*, *The Authoritarian Personality*, New York: Harper and Row, 1950, pp. 281–288.
[19] See Moskos and Bell, *op. cit.*, p. 279. For Jamaica the "white" category includes those leaders who are phenotypically white, but who may be known to have some African ancestry. This type is sometimes referred to as "Jamaican white." For example, see Fernando Henriques, *Jamaica: Land of Wood and Water*, London: Macgibbon and Kee, 1957, p. 131.

with none in levels 5, 6, and 7.[20] The fact that the sample is made up of persons who are more or less prominent public leaders served to restrict the range of variation in occupational levels.

Variation in attitudes toward equality by religious preference gives one particularly clear finding, that is, Protestants were much more likely to favor equality than were Catholics. When party preference was introduced, the relationship was modified only for the JLP and other, with the other Protestant group found to be somewhat less egalitarian than either Anglicans or Roman Catholics. The Anglicans did remain more egalitarian than Catholics, however. Bell also found the Catholics to be the least egalitarian in his 1958 elite study.[21]

Variations on attitudes toward the extension of equality by type of elite position are detailed in Table 15. We see that the elected politicians, and the non-governmental welfare leaders were more

Table 15. **PERCENTAGE OF JAMAICAN LEADERS WHO ARE EGALITARIANS BY TYPE OF ELITE POSITION**

Type of Elite Position	Egalitarians (Per Cent)	No. of Cases on Which the Per Cent is Based
Politicians	71	(21)
Members of Parliament	62	(13)
Parish Councillors	88	(8)
Government Officers	40	(15)
Civil Servants	50	(10)
Jamaica Social Welfare Commission	20	(5)
Non-Governmental Community Welfare Leaders	63	(16)
Clergy	75	(8)
Other	50	(8)

egalitarian than the leaders who were government officers, with the politicians being the highest. This is also true when party is controlled, with the PNP most egalitarian on each type of elite position. While Bell also found the members of the government service to be low on egalitarianism, those elites most comparable to the non-governmental welfare leaders in this study were the most likely to hold egalitarian attitudes and were considerably higher than the elected politicians.[22]

[20] For details of the occupational rating scale see Appendix 2 on Methods.
[21] Bell, *op. cit.*, p. 426.
[22] *Ibid.*

Although few of the differences on attitudes toward equality by social characteristics were large, and most were not uncomplicated by political party preference, the egalitarians were most likely to be young rather than old, more educated than not, black rather than of light skin color, and more were in low occupations than high. Protestants were more often egalitarian than Roman Catholics; and those leaders who preferred the Peoples' National Party were more favorable to egalitarianism than those having other political preferences. Favorable attitudes toward increased equality were underrepresented among the government officers and particularly among leaders who were associated with the Jamaica Social Welfare Commission. This last finding is perhaps the most surprising and disconcerting, since one might, on *a priori* grounds, be led to expect leaders associated with an important welfare agency to be among those committed to the ideal of equality. If the finding is not to be "explained away" by the small number of respondents on which it is based, it raises questions about the effectiveness of social development and welfare staff who as inegalitarians are not in favor of promoting full participation of all Jamaicans in any aspect of society.

EGALITARIANISM AND BELIEF IN PROGRESS

Though attitudes toward equality and progress may be expected to vary together, it need not be so. In the introduction to this chapter, the comments of the British historian, J. B. Bury, served to distinguish the views of Voltaire and Fontenelle from those of Leroux, Condorcet, and Rousseau on this point. We may now proceed to examine this link in Jamaica. Was this association between the belief in progress and the ideal of equality after the Enlightenment tradition to be found among the Jamaican leaders?

The percentage of Jamaican leaders who believed in progress is shown in Table 16 by their attitudes toward equality. Nearly two thirds of those leaders who were egalitarian believed in progress, compared to

Table 16. PERCENTAGE OF JAMAICAN LEADERS WHO BELIEVE IN PROGRESS BY ATTITUDES TOWARD EQUALITY

Attitudes Toward Equality	Percentage Who Believe In Progress	No. of Cases on Which the Per Cent is Based
Egalitarian	65	(31)
Inegalitarian	43	(21)

43 per cent of the inegalitarians. This difference indicates considerable faith in the future well-being of the new nation among those who favor the extension of equality.

This relationship between attitudes toward equality and belief in progress was found not to be spurious when age, education, race-color, occupational rating, religious preference, and political party preference were controlled. Secondarily, there were a few minor refinements of the original relationship.

Such refinements included the fact that the younger egalitarian leaders were more likely to believe in progress than any other age group, and the most educated egalitarians were more likely to believe in progress than the intermediate or the least educated leaders. Although it was shown earlier that the leaders with a high occupational rating were less likely to be egalitarian, when these variables were correlated with belief in progress, it was found that 12 of the 13 high occupation-egalitarians indicated belief in progress. When religious preference was introduced, we found a strong effect of egalitarianism displayed. Within each religious group, egalitarian attitudes were clearly associated with belief in progress. Controlling for political party preference, and thereby to a certain extent for the results of the 1962 election as well, it was found that within each group the egalitarians were more likely to believe in progress than the inegalitarians. However, those egalitarians who preferred the PNP were less likely to see a progressive future for the island than those who were not PNP adherents. Egalitarians who were JLP and "other" were convinced of Jamaica's potential for progress.

On the whole, the relationship between the ideal of equality and belief in progress, which is historically evident in the Enlightenment tradition of thought, was borne out among these leaders in Jamaica. Although the relationship was not strong, those leaders who indicated acceptance of the normative implications of the ideal of equality also were somewhat more likely to hold a vision of a better future for their nation. Their image of a progressive future and their view of the good society tended to include a desired social structure capable of allowing and promoting equal opportunity for full popular participation in all of its aspects. This commitment to equality among these leaders has important and far-reaching implications for other attitudes toward change in Jamaica, because it is one of the important values shaping the images of the future of the nation's social, political, and economic development envisioned by these leaders.

In addition to the conclusion that the ideal of equality inspired the nationalist movements for independence in the West Indies, Moskos and Bell report that egalitarian leaders were more likely than inegalitarians to favor the promotion of a self-conscious and socially inclusive society that emphasized local cultural traditions; they believed more strongly than inegalitarians in the maintenance of representative political democracy and civil rights.[23] The egalitarians believed that a neutralist position in foreign affairs was more consistent with their own concerns for national sovereignty, and they were much *less* likely to favor a Western-oriented foreign policy than were the inegalitarians. Because independence was seen as a means to achieve economic rights for all and a better distribution of economic benefits than was possible under the exploitation of colonial imperialism, it should not be surprising that Moskos and Bell also found the egalitarians to hold more liberal or radical economic ideologies than the inegalitarians. The egalitarians strongly supported a large government role in the economy in order to restructure the economic system and the distribution of resources in favor of the masses of people. From these findings it is clear that the egalitarian ethic is an important component of the ideologies of these new national leaders, and that it should have broad consequences for the future of their nations.

Among the Jamaican leaders, this commitment to equality and a progressive future bodes well for the strengthening of egalitarian political policies which could promote equality of access to education, and allocation of the benefits of development to the widest possible range of Jamaican people. It is only this commitment to equality, when effectively translated into action, that will afford some means to avoid what James S. Coleman has called "the law of unequal development advantage (or disadvantage)." Roughly stated, the law reads that individuals or collectivities that are already more developed have an inherent advantage over those that are less developed.[24] Thus, people who have some greater command over social, economic, and political resources have an advantage in utilizing and promoting further control over those resources. Education is cited as an example which is "... particularly likely to fortify this self-perpetuative propensity among pre-existing inequalities."[25] As a result the process of uneven advancement of individuals, social classes, regions, and even nations tends to be maintained unless the self-reinforcing cycle is disrupted. But it is also possible that full acceptance of the imperatives of equality can create the dilemma that an unrelenting push for equality

---

[23] The findings summarized in this paragraph are from Moskos and Bell, *op. cit.*, passim.
[24] James S. Coleman, "Introduction: Education and Political Development," in James S. Coleman, (ed.), *Education and Political Development*, Princeton, N. J.: Princeton University Press, 1965, p. 31.
[25] *Ibid.*

may seem to work against the capacity of the society for development.[26] According to many Jamaican leaders, their nation is facing this dilemma of the pressure to equalize and democratize Jamaican society and simultaneously to maintain a high level of economic development. As mentioned before, the Jamaican Government's *Five Year Independence Plan, 1963–1968* states that, "The Jamaican situation is a classic demonstration of the race between development and discontent."[27] The critical question of course is whether these goals are necessarily contradictory.

[26] Coleman refers to this as the "equality-capacity dilemma." See *Ibid.*, pp. 31–32, and p. 15.
[27] *Five Year Independence Plan, 1963–1968*, Kingston, Jamaica: Government Printer, 1963, p. 11.

CHAPTER 6 Power and Belief in Progress

Writing about history as fate or decision, C. Wright Mills contended "... that 'men are free to make history' and that some men are now freer than others to do so, for such freedom requires access to the means of decision and of power by which history can now be made." He stated further that, "To assume that men are equally free to make history is to assume that they are equal in power."[1] In accepting Mills' contention we must ask two questions about history-making: First, we must ask about the locus of power, or the distribution of power, that is, "Who is free to make history?", and second, "What shall the nature of that history be?" What are the goals toward which this new history-making is directed? We must ask this second question about ends because that power which is not goal-directed is equivocal in the course it pursues, or expedient in the next step taken. It may be directed toward good or ill, toward the many golden ages past, toward the frustration of all change, or it may be used to lead change and to foster progress. It is precisely here that the role of ideas emerges importantly in the historical process.[2] The impact of ideas upon the course of history increases as men better utilize their resources and increase their power to shape history. In asking what the nature of that history will be, or what course history will take, we must simultaneously ask how power and ideology are associated. For, effective power is that which is joined with ideology; without the guidelines of ideology, power is randomly expended. Power without goals is more easily shunted aside by that which is founded on ideas. Power without

---

[1] C. Wright Mills, *The Causes of World War Three*, New York: Simon and Schuster, 1958, p. 14.
[2] In Max Weber the acceptance of the important role of ideas in history is clearly illustrated, for example, in the role of the Protestant Ethic and later studies of religious ideals in relation to the economy. See Talcott Parsons' introduction to Max Weber, *The Theory of Social and Economic Organization*, trs. Talcott Parsons and A. M. Henderson, Glencoe, Ill.: The Free Press, 1947, p. 6, and p. 123 n. See also Talcott Parsons, "The Role of Ideas in Social Action," in his *Essays in Sociological Theory*, (rev. ed.), Glencoe, Ill.: The Free Press, 1954.

guidelines of action is more easily co-opted by that which is disciplined by adherence to values.

Most of us will agree that ideas may be important determinants of action. But it should also be clear that the role of ideas in social change is not an autonomous one, that the role of ideas depends largely upon the positions in the structures of power held by those who champion the ideas. For this reason we need ask the question concerning the distribution of power.

The consequences of the link between effective power and ideology should be clear. Ideas and power joined as one are important in producing effective action. Witness the fact that we prefer to see power enhanced for those organizations or persons whose ideals we accept, but to see the power of their opposition reduced. We react negatively to the power of the press when it is not guided by an ethic, to the power of the vote not informed by knowledge. We accept the notion that the efficient use of power is directed by ideas, and the goals sought by the powerful are defined and justified by ideology. If these conclusions are valid, they are equally so for ideas with which we agree and accept, as well as for those we reject. Power linked with the ideals of the Enlightenment produced the historic founding of new national states.[3] But also, power linked with the desire to preserve sectional interests and the privilege of a ruling minority have perpetuated white Rhodesian and South African nationalism. Power linked with ideas of Aryan superiority produced the evil efficacy of mass genocide. Power linked with ideas of racial inferiority have maintained a system of profitable exploitation of people. An awareness of the associations between power and ideology is a prerequisite to thinking about what the nature of history shall be. So we shall ask how power is related to the ideals which constitute the core of this research, and whether the command of power itself affects the alternative courses of action considered, the goals chosen, and the plans made for their attainment?

The relative amount of power held by particular Jamaican leaders and the ideals linked with that power are the focus of this chapter. An Index of Power is presented and the distribution of power among these leaders is described. Power is then examined in the context of the ideas which may direct and legitimate its use. Specifically, variation in belief in progress among the Jamaican leaders is analyzed in terms of the

---

[3] See Charles C. Moskos, Jr., *The Sociology of Political Independence: A Study of Nationalist Attitudes Among West Indian Leaders,* Cambridge, Mass.: Schenkman Publishing Co., 1967.

relative power of these leaders. This relationship is elaborated by the introduction of attitudes toward equality.

AN INDEX OF POWER

Power is participation in the decision-making process including the determination and implementation of policy.[4] With this definition as a point of departure, it is here asserted that those persons who are frequently nominated as important in determining and implementing policy are likely to have more power than those who are mentioned less frequently or not mentioned at all. Thus, each Jamaican leader was asked:

> Now, I'd like you to tell me the names of the people you think are most important in determining and carrying out policy in relation to the problems of West Kingston.

This question served both to define the universe of leaders relevant to the urban lower-class area and as the basis for the Index of Power.[5] This index is made up of two components. The first is simply a reputational power score computed for each individual on the basis of the number of nominations he received in response to the above question. But, it is clear that such a reputation for power need not imply effective power. The reputation of being powerful may stem from a history of effective action toward given goals, or from the position a person occupies, or both. Because reputational measures of power may result in a confounding of effective power with positionally derived potential for power, a second component was included in the Index of Power. This second indicator is a score for each individual leader representing his knowledge about the power of other leaders. This component of the index rests on the assumption that effective participation in the decision-making process, that is, the possession of power, will be associated with relatively more accurate and complete knowledge of the system of power relations relevant to the issues in question. Those who are more powerful will have more accurate and complete knowledge of the identity of others who participate effectively in the decision-making process. Thus, this second

---

[4] This definition is drawn from Harold D. Lasswell and Abraham Kaplan, *Power and Society: A Framework for Political Inquiry*, New Haven: Yale University Press, 1950, pp. 74–75.

[5] The relevance of the multitude of criticisms of the reputational approach to the study of community power is discussed in Appendix 1 on methods; for a discussion of the reputational approach to the study of leadership, see Wendell Bell, Richard J. Hill, and Charles R. Wright, *Public Leadership*, San Francisco: Chandler Publishing Company, 1961, Chapter II.

component of the Index of Power may be thought of as a correction factor which reduces the contribution of reputational power derived from formal position alone in the composite index.[6]

The designation of leaders as *relatively* more or less powerful in public affairs relating to West Kingston is systematically based on their *reputation for power* and their *knowledge of the relative power of others*. These two components of the index were combined and the resulting scores were dichotomized at the median interval. As a consequence of this dichotomous treatment of the index scores, 51 per cent of the leaders were classified as most powerful.[7]

SOCIAL DIFFERENTIATION AND POWER

The distribution of power in public affairs regarding West Kingston among these leaders is presented by selected social characteristics in Table 17. As might be expected, the adherents of the government party, the JLP, had the largest percentage classified as most powerful, and the leaders with no clearly determined party preference had the smallest percentage so classified. About half of the leaders aligned with the opposition party, the PNP, were categorized as relatively powerful, compared to seven out of ten of the leaders aligned with the ruling JLP. In addition, there were sizeable differences in the relative power of the leaders by age groups. Two thirds of the younger leaders, those under 40 years of age, were among the most powerful, compared to just over one third of the leaders over fifty years old, with the middle-age group falling in between. Among both the JLP- and PNP-aligned leaders, those under fifty years of age were more likely to be classified as powerful than those over fifty. However, for those with no clear party preference this relationship with age was reversed. For the total universe of leaders the overall finding that more of the relatively powerful leaders were among the younger persons than the older group is not surprising when it is considered in the light of other information. For example, four of the JLP Cabinet Ministers were under forty years of age at the time of the study, and all of them were classified as "most powerful." Moreover, the general finding that

---

[6] This use of the knowledge of the power of others is not unlike that of Foskett and Hohle in their community power research. They correlated reputational nominations with the knowledge of the power structure. See John M. Foskett and Raymond Hohle, "The Measurement of Influence in Community Affairs," *Proceedings of the Pacific Sociological Society, Research Studies of the State College of Washington*, XXV (June, 1957), pp. 148–154.

[7] Details of computation are to be found in Appendix 2 on Methods. For ease of discussion the measure will be referred to as the *Index of Power*, and the high-scoring leaders as relatively more powerful, but the reader should be reminded that it refers to power ascertained by a reputational measure.

Table 17. PERCENTAGE OF JAMAICAN LEADERS WHO ARE MOST POWERFUL BY SELECTED SOCIAL CHARACTERISTICS

Selected Characteristic	Most Powerful (Per Cent)	No. of Cases on Which the Per Cent is Based
Political Party Preference		
Jamaica Labour Party	69	(13)
Peoples' National Party	52	(25)
Other	33	(15)
Age		
50 and older	37	(19)
40–49	55	(22)
39 and younger	67	(12)
Education		
University or college graduate	50	(16)
Some university or college	56	(9)
Secondary school or less	50	(28)
Race–color		
White	57	(14)
Brown	54	(13)
Black	46	(26)
Occupational Rating		
1 (Highest)	56	(27)
2–4 (Lowest)	46	(26)
Religious Preference		
Anglican	67	(15)
Other Protestant	73	(15)
Roman Catholic	43	(7)
Jewish	—	(1)

younger persons are most frequently classified as powerful is consistent with the focus on power relevant to an issue that is limited in scope and defined by a limited area.

Although there were only slight differences in power associated with differing levels of education, these effects were manifested in contradictory ways for the two parties, and those with no clear party preference. Among the leaders who favored the PNP, a monotonic increase in the percentage classified as most powerful was associated with increasing level of formal education. For those aligned with the governing JLP there was very little relationship between their education and whether they were classified as relatively powerful. However, for those persons with no clear political sentiments, the relationship was reversed with the most educated falling into the least powerful group, and the least educated more frequently in the most powerful group of leaders. This is accounted for by the fact that the religious leaders interviewed were most often highly educated, usually expressed no particular political preference, and were classified as relatively less powerful.

The distribution of power by race-color shows the white leaders more likely to be most powerful than the black leaders, with the brown-skinned persons in the intermediate position. These differences were clear, but not large. When party preference was controlled, the whites were still found more often than black-skinned leaders in the most powerful category, but of the six subgroup comparisons of color by party, the brown-skinned PNP adherents were most frequent among the powerful, and the brown JLP and other group were the least frequent. Some of these findings must certainly be attributed to covariation of party preference and type of elite position held by the leaders.

Differences in relative power of the leaders by their occupational level were not large, and were little affected by variation in party preference. Regardless of political alignment, those of high occupational rating were more likely to be rated as powerful than those with low rated occupations. These differences might have been larger if the distribution of occupations was not skewed in favor of the higher ratings.

Anglicans and other Protestants were considerably more often classified as powerful than adherents to Roman Catholicism. This finding for Catholic leaders was also true when political party preference was controlled.

Additional data are given in Table 18. There, the percentage of leaders who were classified as most powerful are shown by type of

Table 18. PERCENTAGE OF JAMAICAN LEADERS WHO ARE MOST POWERFUL BY TYPE OF ELITE POSITION

Type of Elite Position	Most Powerful (Per Cent)	No. of Cases on Which the Per Cent is Based
Politicians	60	(20)
Members of Parliament	75	(12)
Parish Councillors	38	(8)
Government Officers	50	(16)
Civil Servants	50	(10)
Jamaica Social Welfare Commission	50	(6)
Non-Governmental Community Welfare Leaders	41	(17)
Clergy	33	(9)
Other	50	(8)

elite position. While there are clear differences between the three general categories of politicians, government officers, and non-governmental leaders, the largest differences in the table are between the specific types of leadership roles. The group most frequently rated as most powerful were the Members of Parliament. The Parish Councillors and clergy were the least likely to be relatively powerful, with the government officers and others holding the intermediate position.

POWER, EQUALITY, AND PROGRESS

We may now proceed to the examination of the ideological context within which the possession of power must be considered. First, can we expect the power of Jamaican leaders to be directed toward the achievement of future progress? And, to what extent shall the ideal of equality guide the use of that power in its direction of change. We have seen in Chapter 5 that egalitarian leaders were most likely to believe in progress. We may now ascertain whether access to the means of decision contributed to the frequency of such beliefs among these leaders.

The first of these questions is answered in Table 19. There, the percentage of leaders who believed in progress is given by the Index of Power. It would seem that the less powerful leaders were somewhat

Table 19. **PERCENTAGE OF JAMAICAN LEADERS WHO BELIEVE IN PROGRESS BY THE INDEX OF POWER**

Index of Power	Percentage Who Believe In Progress	No. of Cases on Which the Per Cent is Based
Most powerful	63	(27)
Least powerful	46	(26)

less confident than the most powerful leaders in facing the obstacles presented by the future. Forty-six per cent of the less powerful leaders believed in progress compared to 63 per cent of those who were most powerful. This relationship remained with few exceptions when the variables presented in Table 17 were controlled. This difference was found not to be spurious when age, race-color, occupational rating, and political party alignment of the leaders were each introduced. The relationship between power and belief in progress remained also among those leaders with some college or university training and those with secondary education or less. It was found, however, that among the university graduates the least powerful leaders were most likely to believe in progress. Examined in the light of type of elite position of the leaders, it becomes apparent that the religious leaders were again the "deviant" cases. They are typically highly educated and likely to believe in progress irrespective of their relatively low power.

Although the partial correlation by religious preference did not confirm the initial relationship between power and belief in progress, it is also true that this particular comparison is not reliable because of the clearly non-random distribution of those leaders for whom there was no information concerning their religious preference. Nearly two thirds of them had low scores on the Index of Power and were doubtful about the island's potential for progress. Finally, the relationship between power and belief in progress when compared within each type of elite was reversed only for the non-governmental community welfare leaders. The clergy discussed above comprised nearly half of this group.

On the whole, there seems to be adequate grounds for accepting the correlation between power and belief in progress as not spurious. The percentage difference, though not large, clearly reveals that relationship. But, first, we must ask whether or not the contribution of power to variations in belief in progress was independent of the correlation with egalitarian attitudes. We saw in Table 16 that those leaders who were egalitarian were likely to believe in progress. This three-variable relationship is presented in Table 20.

Table 20. PERCENTAGE OF JAMAICAN LEADERS WHO BELIEVE IN PROGRESS BY ATTITUDES TOWARD EQUALITY AND THE INDEX OF POWER

Egalitarianism and Index of Power	Percentage Who Believe In Progress	No. of Cases on Which the Per Cent is Based
Egalitarian and most powerful	73	(15)
Egalitarian and least powerful	53	(15)
Inegalitarian and most powerful	50	(12)
Inegalitarian and least powerful	33	(9)

Consideration of the percentages in Table 20 reveals that both egalitarianism and power contributed toward belief in progress independently of one another. Among those leaders who were egalitarian and powerful 73 per cent were committed to the notion of future progress, compared to 33 per cent of the leaders who were both inegalitarian and least powerful. There was no difference between the least powerful egalitarians and the powerful inegalitarians. About half of each group believed in progress.

Let us speculate briefly about the implications of these findings for the future of Jamaica and of the urban lower classes in particular. What shall the nature of their future history be? May we expect progressive development of human potential? May we expect increasing knowledge, material resources, and control over the social and technological environments? It was argued in Chapter 2 that some of the major trends of change in Jamaica's recent past have been progressive. The rapid economic development of the island and the trend toward equality of opportunity and social inclusiveness serve as examples. Possibly I have overstressed the achievements in this regard; or perhaps when considered against the background of Jamaica's early colonial history these achievements underscore themselves. In either case, the potential for further progress should not be minimized.

It has been shown that those leaders most likely to believe in progress were those who were relatively more powerful and committed to the ideal of the egalitarian society. If the assumptions made here about the role of ideas in history-making, particularly ideas articulated by men of power, are justified, we will see many of the past progressive trends of change receive support from more and larger segments of Jamaican society. But, if those leaders capable of influence shed their egalitarian ideology and abdicate their responsibility, whether out of self-interest or despair, we may see those progressive trends falter. These words of Mills are again appropriate in his conclusion that, ". . . those who have access to the new means of power, and yet define their situation as one of fate — do they not stand now in objective default?"[8]

[8] Mills, *op. cit.*, p. 14.

CHAPTER 7 Knowledge and Belief in Progress

In stressing the importance of the link between egalitarian ideals and power among the leaders who believe in progress, I have said little about the role of sheer knowledge. It was noted that power alone was insufficient without goals or guidelines for action. What is needed is an ideal or ideology. Although knowledge has been implicitly included in the discussion, particularly in reference to decision-making, there has been no clear demonstration of its importance.

Like many other societies entering the modern world, Jamaica is becoming a society in which the state of the society, economy, and polity are potentially amenable to history-making by conscious decision. The impact of ideologies on the course of history is made possible by their union with power as important foundations of effective action. Knowledge is a third element of critical importance in the conscious determination of future history because facts, along with values and expectations, are the basic components of the decision-making process by which the future is shaped.[1] Kenneth Boulding has said that it is only by means of knowledge ". . . that we can hope to understand the social system sufficiently well to be able to control it and to be able to move into a positive image of the future through our own volition and policy."[2]

The feasibility of planning the desirable future increases as our knowledge of the facts and conditions of society increases. Without knowledge, directed change and the planned future are impossible; with insufficient knowledge, ". . . we are merely slaves of necessity or victims of chance."[3]

The purpose of this chapter is to make explicit the role of the leaders' knowledge in relation to their belief in progress. An Index

[1] Heinz Eulau, "H. D. Lasswell's Developmental Analysis," *The Western Political Quarterly*, XI (June, 1958), p. 230.
[2] Kenneth Boulding, "The Relations of Economic, Political and Social Systems," *Social and Economic Studies*, XI (December, 1962), pp. 358–359.
[3] *Ibid.*, p. 359.

of Knowledge is constructed and the distribution of knowledgeable leaders by social characteristics is described. We then turn to the assessment of the importance of knowledge for belief in progress, and see how knowledge is integrated in the matrix of relationships with power, egalitarianism, and belief in progress.

The knowledge we are concerned with in this chapter, like the universe of leaders, was defined as *knowledge about the urban lower classes and West Kingston*. The leaders, it will be remembered, were all persons responsible, in some measure, for the betterment of the social and physical milieu of these people. They should have considerable knowledge of the West Kingston residents. But it has been said that elites in most underdeveloped countries do not usually have knowledge of the poor or the subculture created by poverty.[4] To what extent was this true in Jamaica? Were the leaders knowledgeable about the people whose conditions of life they were supposed to improve? And, most importantly, how did the possession of knowledge affect the likelihood that the leaders would believe in Jamaica's future potential?

One of the important and paradoxical features of West Kingston is its simultaneous invisibility and prominence. A West Indian novelist has remarked that in "the Jamaican middle-class world . . . almost by design, it appears — that one can move from suburb to suburb and never cease to be sheltered from offending sights."[5] To see the Jamaica that is West Kingston you have to look. "And once you start looking, you can see nothing else."[6] Among those who don't look, West Kingston has been the object of heedless indifference. Yet, for some who look, its prominence has given rise to fear and antipathy. West Kingston is rarely thought of as a problem for the people who live there, but rather as a threat to the stability of the country, and to the health and longevity of fair-skinned women and children. We must here ask if these community leaders thought of the area in terms of the problems of the people there, or were they ignorant of the interests and needs of the people of West Kingston. In either case, what were the consequences for their belief or disbelief in progress?

AN INDEX OF KNOWLEDGE

The Index of Knowledge is a measure of the accuracy and completeness of the leaders' knowledge of the complaints and discontents of

---

[4] Oscar Lewis, *Five Families*, New York: Basic Books, Inc., 1959, p. 2.
[5] V. S. Naipaul, *The Middle Passage*, London: Andre Deutsch, 1962, p. 215.
[6] *Ibid.*, p. 216.

the lower-class people who reside in West Kingston. The leaders were asked:

> What specific discontents and complaints are fairly widespread among the people of West Kingston?

A similar question was asked of the sample of lower-class residents of the area. The responses of both leaders and lower-class respondents were recorded in detail and compared. The measure of the leaders' knowledge is based on the amount of agreement with the discontents reported by the people themselves, as determined by the West Kingston sample survey. For mentioning the "correct" problems and discontents, the leaders were scored in proportion to the frequency of those complaints in the responses of the lower classes. The resulting distribution of scores was dichotomized at that interval which created the most homogeneous groupings according to the level of knowledge.[7] In the percentage distribution of leaders according to the Index of Knowledge of the discontents of the West Kingston people, 63 per cent were classified as most knowledgeable about the needs and problems of this lower-class area; the remaining 37 per cent were classified as relatively less knowledgeable. Although this index does not measure the leaders' knowledge of the problems of the urban lower classes in any absolute sense, it does provide an indication of their knowledge relative to one another.

This index and the question on which it is based ought not to be thought of as a simple variant of social distance or the amount of contact the leaders had with the people of the area. The attribution of high contact to the knowledgeable and low contact to those of little knowledge is not valid in many cases. It seems that contact with the people was not a sufficient condition for being knowledgeable about their discontents. This conclusion is based both on my personal observations and on data from the interviews. I would suggest that attitudes toward the lower-class people served to shape the results of contact upon the level of knowledge. For example, an inegalitarian leader who perceived lower-class persons to be lazy may accordingly reinterpret the complaints he hears, or he may simply reject them as meaningless, regardless of the amount of contact he has with them.

---

[7] For the details of the method by which this index was constructed see Appendix 2. This distribution was such that dichotomizing at the median would have resulted in the combination of persons with radically divergent scores. For this reason it was divided at a point above the median where the scores designated as high and low were most homogeneous within categories.

SOCIAL DIFFERENTIATION AND KNOWLEDGE

The percentages of leaders who were most knowledgeable are specified in Table 21 by selected social characteristics. There was little variation in knowledge of lower-class discontents by age. A slight

Table 21. PERCENTAGE OF JAMAICAN LEADERS WHO ARE MOST KNOWLEDGEABLE BY SELECTED SOCIAL CHARACTERISTICS

Selected Characteristic	Most Knowledgeable (Per Cent)	No. of Cases on Which the Per Cent is Based
Political Party Preference		
Jamaica Labour Party	46	(13)
Peoples' National Party	65	(26)
Other	73	(15)
Age		
50 and over	65	(20)
40–49	64	(22)
39 and under	58	(12)
Education		
University or college graduate	71	(17)
Some university or college	78	(9)
Secondary school or less	54	(28)
Race–color		
White	64	(14)
Brown	57	(14)
Black	65	(26)
Occupational Rating		
1 (Highest)	61	(28)
2–4 (Lowest)	65	(26)
Religion		
Anglican	80	(15)
Other Protestant	50	(16)
Roman Catholic	57	(7)
Jewish	—	(1)

tendency for older leaders to be among the most knowledegable was evident among the leaders of JLP and other category, but there was no difference in knowledge by age among the leaders who preferred the PNP.

Differences in knowledge by educational level, religious preference, and political party are the only large differences in Table 21. Generally, those who had more formal education were also more likely than the least educated group to be classified as most knowledgeable about the discontents of the West Kingston people. The increase by education was not monotonic, however. The leaders with at least some university or college training were the most knowledgeable group, while those in the lowest educational category were the least knowledgeable. The difference between the most and least educated was sizeable, and increased for the leaders who were not aligned with the PNP. But among those who preferred the PNP, the most educated were most often less knowledgeable, while those with some university or college training were likely to be in the most knowledgeable group. Those leaders who were Anglicans were clearly among the most knowledgeable, followed by the Roman Catholics, and then by other Protestants. This relationship between religious preference and the leaders' relative knowledge remained consistent when political party preference was introduced.

There were only slight variations in amount of knowledge by race-color, and by occupational rating. Differences by race-color were little affected by controlling for political party preference, but among the PNP-aligned leaders, the brown persons were the least knowledgeable. This one comparison showed a sizeable difference. Also, the slight tendency for the low occupational group to be more knowledgeable was magnified among the JLP and other sub-group.

The percentage of Jamaican leaders who were most knowledgeable is shown in Table 22 by the type of elite position they occupied. By far the most knowledgeable group of leaders were the government

Table 22. **PERCENTAGE OF JAMAICAN LEADERS WHO ARE MOST KNOWLEDGEABLE BY TYPE OF ELITE POSITION**

Type of Elite Position	Most Knowledgeable (Per Cent)	No. of Cases on Which the Per Cent is Based
Politicians	52	(21)
Members of Parliament	46	(13)
Parish Councillors	63	(8)
Government Officers	81	(16)
Civil Servants	80	(10)
Jamaica Social Welfare Commission	83	(6)
Non-Governmental Community Welfare Leaders	59	(17)
Clergy	67	(9)
Other	50	(8)

officers, including the civil servants and members of the Jamaica Welfare Commission staff. Eighty-one per cent of these government officers were knowledgeable. Next, 59 per cent of the non-governmental community welfare leaders had knowledge of the discontents of the lower class in Western Kingston. The politicians were low in knowledge, with the Members of Parliament having the lowest figure in the table. Forty-six per cent were knowledgeable. Most of these were JLP members from rural areas, since in recent years the PNP has maintained control of the constituencies in the Kingston metropolitan area. Therefore, it is not too surprising to find them lacking knowledge of the specific discontents of the urban lower classes. Among the politicians, the members of the Kingston-St. Andrew Corporation, the local government agency, were somewhat more knowledgeable with 63 per cent so classified. Each of these relationships between knowledge and type of elite position remained when party preference was introduced.

KNOWLEDGE AND BELIEF IN PROGRESS

The percentage of Jamaican leaders who believed in progress is given in Table 23 by the level of knowledge about the discontents of the urban lower classes. It is clear that belief in progress is positively

Table 23. PERCENTAGE OF JAMAICAN LEADERS WHO BELIEVE IN PROGRESS BY THE INDEX OF KNOWLEDGE

Index of Knowledge	Percentage Who Believe in Progress	No. of Cases on Which the Per Cent is Based
High knowledge	62	(34)
Low knowledge	45	(20)

associated with knowledge. Sixty-two per cent of the leaders who were knowledgeable were committed to the notion of progress, compared to 45 per cent of those leaders who were low on the Index of Knowledge. This correlation remained when party preference, race-color, religious preference, and type of elite position were introduced as controls.

When age was introduced, the original relationship between knowledge and belief in progress vanished among those leaders in the oldest age group, and the difference was increased among those leaders aged 40 to 49 years. There was no difference in belief in progress by level of knowledge for the leaders who were low on education. Generally, the more educated leaders who had knowledge of the interests and needs of the lower-class people of West Kingston were likely to believe in progress. There was no difference in belief in progress by knowledge among the lower occupational levels, while the difference among the higher-status leaders was considerably magnified.

While it was shown in Table 21 that the leaders who were Roman Catholic were not too likely to be knowledgeable, it was found here that in every case, those Catholics who were knowledgeable believed in progress. This was also true for all the clergy regardless of denomination; those who were knowledgeable believed in progress. Similarly, among the Members of Parliament it was found that 46 per cent were knowledgeable, but 83 per cent of the knowledgeable believed in progress.

From these data we may conclude that belief in progress is not an uninformed idealism that should be relegated simply to the realm of utopian fantasy. It is based on a realistic awareness of the demands of the urban lower classes. Perhaps it is knowledge of the lower-class people as a resource to be developed and drawn upon as a force for national progress, and not merely a knowledge of their complaints and discontents that supports their belief in the island's potential. This assumes, of course, that those leaders who have knowledge of the deficiencies in the society's provisions for the lower classes, and of the resulting discontents, will also be aware of the strengths that recommend these people as a resource to be mobilized for the more rapid development of the nation. If this interpretation is valid, then the contribution of knowledge to belief in progress would not be based solely on the knowledge of discontents arising from the incapability to provide acceptable minimums for all, but upon the positive evaluations of these peoples' potential.

KNOWLEDGE, POWER, AND EGALITARIANISM

The two preceding chapters each provided a partial answer to questions about the framework within which belief in progress must be considered. We saw the ideology of egalitarianism was related to belief in progress. The Index of Power developed in Chapter 6 showed that access to the forums of decision contributed to belief in progress. In addition, it was demonstrated in Table 19 that both power and attitudes toward equality contributed independently to belief in progress. Finally, we have just seen that belief in progress was not a blind and unrealistic idealism founded on blissful ignorance. Rather, it tended toward the reverse. Those leaders who were ignorant of the problems of the urban lower classes were not likely to affirm the progressive character of social change in Jamaica's future compared to more knowledgeable leaders. We may now determine whether or not this contribution of knowledge to belief in progress was independent of egalitarianism and power.

In Table 24 the contribution of knowledge to belief in progress is shown to be separable from that of attitudes toward equality. Each of these variables serves to predict a different and additional part of the variance in belief in progress. Those leaders who were knowledgeable

Table 24. PERCENTAGE OF JAMAICAN LEADERS WHO BELIEVE IN PROGRESS BY THE INDEX OF KNOWLEDGE AND ATTITUDES TOWARD EQUALITY

Index of Knowledge and Egalitarianism	Percentage Who Believe in Progress	No. of Cases on Which the Per Cent is Based
Knowledgeable and egalitarian	70	(23)
Knowledgeable and inegalitarian	40	(10)
Not knowledgeable and egalitarian	50	(8)
Not knowledgeable and inegalitarian	45	(11)

and egalitarian were more likely to believe in progress than any other combination of those variables. Seventy per cent of those leaders who were high on the Index of Knowledge and who were favorable to the extension of equality in Jamaica believed in the island's potential for progress. At the other extreme, 45 per cent of those who were inegalitarian and had little knowledge of the people of West Kingston indicated belief in progress.

Three of the four comparisons to be made in Table 24 confirm the expectations based on the simple two variable relationships. The one unexpected finding is that slightly more of the leaders who were low on knowledge and also inegalitarian believed in progress than did the knowledgeable inegalitarians. This difference was small, however.

The association between belief in progress, knowledge, and power is given in Table 25. There it becomes even more clear that knowledge contributes independently to the understanding of variation in belief

Table 25. PERCENTAGE OF JAMAICAN LEADERS WHO BELIEVE IN PROGRESS BY THE INDEX OF KNOWLEDGE AND THE INDEX OF POWER

Index of Knowledge and Index of Power	Percentage Who Believe in Progress	No. of Cases on Which the Per Cent is Based
Knowledgeable and most powerful	72	(18)
Knowledgeable and least powerful	50	(16)
Not knowledgeable and most powerful	44	(9)
Not knowledgeable and least powerful	40	(10)

in progress. Those leaders who were most knowledgeable and most powerful were most likely to believe in progress. Of that group, 72 per cent indicated belief in progress compared to 40 per cent of those who were low on both the Index of Knowledge and the Index of Power. Half of the knowledgeable but least powerful leaders believed in progress, and 44 per cent of those with low knowledge, yet powerful, held that view of the future. Each comparison is as expected. When knowledge is held constant, the powerful leaders more often believed in progress. Similarly, when power is controlled the frequency of belief in progress is higher among the leaders with more knowledge.

Following the same logic of analysis with which we have come thus far, the next step is the determination of the cumulative effect of egalitarian attitudes, power in the affairs of West Kingston, and knowledge of the discontents of the people there, simultaneously, upon variation in belief in progress. For this purpose a multi-dimensional index of these three variables was constructed. The measures of each of these variables, as dichotomies, were combined in a configuration of greater complexity which would allow the simultaneous elaboration of the relationship between these three independent variables and belief in progress.[8] Scores of zero or one were given to the leaders on each of the three variables. Zeros were assigned to inegalitarian attitudes, to low scores on the Index of Power, and to low scores on the Index of Knowledge. The categories given a one point value were conversely, egalitarian attitudes, high power score, and high knowledge score. The sum of these three assigned values is the total score on the composite index. Therefore, the highest possible score was three, and the lowest zero.[9]

Table 26. PERCENTAGE OF JAMAICAN LEADERS WHO BELIEVE IN PROGRESS BY THE COMPOSITE INDEX OF EGALITARIANISM, POWER, AND KNOWLEDGE

Composite Index Scores	Percentage Who Believe in Progress	No. of Cases on Which the Per Cent is Based
3 (Highest)	82	(11)
2	57	(23)
0–1 (Lowest)	33	(18)

Having constructed the index, we may now look at the cumulative effect of this configurational variable upon the Jamaican leaders' belief in progress. The percentage of leaders who believe in progress is

[8] See Herbert Hyman's discussion of the deliberate creation of a configuration which, though synthetic, allows more complex and refined analysis; *Survey Design and Analysis*, Glencoe, Ill.: The Free Press, 1955, pp. 271–272.

[9] Without any doubt it would be desirable to continue this analysis by means of the four-variable table that would logically follow. But, unfortunately, the small number of cases on which the analysis is based would yield less than reliable correlations. Rather than be thwarted by this and stop at this point it was decided to proceed by means of this composite index.

presented in Table 26 by the composite index of egalitarianism, power, and knowledge. Eighty-two per cent of the leaders who were egalitarian, powerful, and knowledgeable (score 3) believed in progress. At the opposite extreme we find that a third of those who were assigned low scores (0 or 1) on the composite index, believed in Jamaica's potential for progress.[10] Score 2 contained 57 per cent who believed in progress.

Comparison of the highest categories in Tables 24, 25, and 26 shows that each of the three variables in the composite index makes an additional and independent contribution to the prediction of belief in progress. Seventy per cent of those who were both knowledgeable and egalitarian (Table 24), and 72 per cent of those who were knowledgeable and powerful (Table 25) were leaders who indicated a belief in Jamaica's future progress. The percentage who held such beliefs is raised to 82 per cent (Table 26) by the simultaneous consideration of all three of the predicting variables. In sum, those leaders who were egalitarian, powerful, and knowledgeable were more likely to believe in progress than those who did not favor equality, who were relatively powerless, and who were ignorant of the specific interests and the needs of the people for whom and to whom they were responsible.

[10] The zero and one scores were combined in Table 26, because of the small number of cases in the low-scored cells of the table. It should be noted however, that the inegalitarian, least powerful, and least knowledgeable leaders (score zero) were more likely to believe in progress than predicted. Even though it is possible that this reversal is not spurious, the size and consistency of differences in this and preceding tables warrant general confidence in the conclusions drawn from Table 26 as it is presented.

CHAPTER 8 The Myth of the Hostile Masses

In 1965, Jamaicans marked the centennial of the Morant Bay Rebellion. It was an incident hardly deserving the name "rebellion": it was not part of a general insurrection, nor was it an uprising against the white oligarchy. A militant band of St. Thomas hill-people, intent on airing their grievances, marched to Morant Bay to confront the administration. In the rioting that followed, a handful of the black rioters and perhaps 21 other persons were killed. The official reaction to the incident by the Governor, Edward John Eyre, was brutally vengeful. Six hundred "rebels" were flogged and nearly as many killed.[1] This violent reaction effectively "pacified" the parish of St. Thomas, but probably did little to allay the fears of the ruling minority.

In April, 1963, Jamaicans heard by radio broadcast of another "uprising," this time involving six Ras Tafarians on the North Coast of the island. Reminiscent of the Morant Bay disturbance of 1865, the nature of the incident was misjudged. It was most certainly not an uprising, yet the misnomer was quickly applied. The repressive official reaction in the hours and days that followed, although less severe, was also reminiscent of Governor Eyre and Morant Bay. The Prime Minister called out the Chief of Staff of the Jamaica Defense Force; troops, armed police, armored cars, and Cabinet Ministers rushed to Montego Bay. Hundreds of persons, some Ras Tafarians, others simply black men with beards, were imprisoned or denied their freedom temporarily.[2] Reports of police brutality during this roundup were frequent.[3] Yet, this was occurring even while it was known that the six "Rastas" involved in the incident had either been killed, captured, or were elsewhere in the district. One can only surmise that this repressive reaction

[1] J. H. Parry and P. M. Sherlock, *A Short History of the West Indies*, London: MacMillan and Co., Ltd., 1957, p. 241.
[2] *Daily Gleaner*, April 13, 1963, p. 1; *Newday*, VII (April, 1963), p. 14; *Spotlight*, XXIV (April–May, 1963), p. 17; *The Star*, Kingston, April 13, 1963, p. 12.
[3] *Public Opinion*, XXVII (June 7, 1963), p. 4.

to a purely local incident grew out of fear and the belief that others among the depressed and poor might heed the example given by some criminals in the "lunatic fringe." What other reason could explain the mass arrests? Vengeance? Probably not. Rather, the reaction was probably intended to intimidate any others who might be a threat to order and stability, and to put to rest the easily aroused fears of many Jamaicans who viewed the lower social orders as malevolent and barbaric.

To many Jamaicans, this popular image of the black masses as hostile would not seem unreasonable or unfounded. It is an image supported by objective conditions of social and economic life in Jamaica. Who should be more aware of the improvements in levels of living than the burgeoning middle and upper classes to whom the benefits of Jamaica's development have largely accrued? But some of them are also aware of the vast disparities in the distribution of those benefits. Although the lessening of inequalities of minimum rights of all Jamaicans has been an important trend, it remains clearly evident that gross inequalities of opportunity and achievement are widespread. The level of living among the lower classes is certainly not desirable. The maldistribution of income, the level of unemployment, the rising cost of living, the lack of educational opportunities, the lack of adequate housing, and inadequate social services are only a few of the acknowledged deficiencies. Moreover, those shortcomings are magnified in the urban areas due to the pressure of sheer numbers. Awareness of these conditions obviously buttresses the middle- and upper-class Jamaicans' belief in the hostility of his less fortunate countrymen.

In addition to these objective conditions of deprivation of the lower classes, support for the belief that they are at war with the middle and upper classes may be found in the styles of thought concerning social relationships among the various social classes. For example, I have already mentioned, in another context, the comment of a government officer who publicly declared that the condition of the lower classes "constituted a peril that might erupt at any time." Comparable sentiments have been expressed by a writer who remarked that "Nervous people sipping Scotch by the poinsettias on their patios have asked one another how long they will be safe in their beds."[4] National elections and the advent of independence occasioned the heightening of these sentiments. There were frequent rumors in Jamaica and abroad that the elections of 1962 would be accompanied by widespread eruptions of violence. The "scaremongers," as the local press dubbed them, suggested that Jamaica was in an explosive state and would soon become

---

[4] Marjorie Hughes, *The Fairest Island*, London: Victor Gollancz, Ltd., 1962, p. 12.

another Cuba.⁵ In the weeks preceding the celebration of Jamaica's independence, there were persistent rumors of forthcoming violence. In mid-July, one columnist wrote:

> A man would have had to be stone deaf not to have caught the most blood-curdling rumours, during the last few weeks, of violence brewing for Independence Day. Promises of bloodshed, rape and untrammeled looting are offered to you with anticipatory relish, by people who should know much better.⁶

The article goes on to mention that "according to all the best informed verandah gossips," all the local stores had sold out their stock of machetes to persons seeking weapons for the coming bloodbath. Indeed, this fantastic story became the subject of legislative commentary by the Hon. N.N. Ashenheim, Leader of Government Business in the Legislative Council. In a story headlined, "ASHENHEIM: NO TRUTH ABOUT JUMP IN MACHETE-BUYING," *The Daily Gleaner* reported that Mr. Ashenheim said, ". . . there was no truth at all in the rumour that people were buying machetes to start a revolution in the island during the independence celebrations."⁷ This was shortly followed by the Government's declaration in the Legislative Council and to the people of Jamaica that elaborate arrangements had been prepared for the maintenance of law and order during independence, and that it would be a grave error for anyone to underestimate the effectiveness of these precautions.⁸

In addition, it has also been in vogue among middle- and upper-class persons discussing Jamaica's development, to lay heavy stress on the problem of the "revolution of rising expectations among the masses." Similarly, it was fashionable to point to the conservatism of organized labor, especially among those workers called by one Jamaican economist, "the labor elite." These more prosperous workers seem to establish their self-identification with the middle class by moralizing about the behavior of the less fortunate masses, and negating any association with them.⁹ These people feed on and foster the stereotype of the masses as harboring dangerous animosity toward the rest of society.

Another facet of this phenomenon may stem from an important influence in the heritage of modern social and political thought; namely,

---

⁵ See *The Star*, Kingston, Jamaica, April 16, 1962.
⁶ See "Violence and Independence," in *The Daily Gleaner*, Kingston, Jamaica, July 15, 1962.
⁷ *The Daily Gleaner*, Monday, July 9, 1962.
⁸ *Ibid.*
⁹ M. G. Smith, "The Plural Framework of Jamaican Society," *The British Journal of Sociology*, XII (September, 1961), p. 261.

Marxism and the radical tradition. This tradition of thought promotes an interpretation of history and a definition of the current situation that supports the belief that the lower classes are in conflict with the middle and upper classes. Even the loudest anti-communists among Jamaican politicians view the lower classes with an eye on their revolutionary potential. Jamaica's confrontation with the experience of Haiti and the republics in and around the Caribbean basin lends credibility to their fears of lower-class antagonism. A fear of *Fidelismo* and any other movement of an ideological nature directed at the lower orders has resulted. [10]

In brief, the stereotypes conveyed by the press, the styles of thought regarding the relations between classes, and the objective conditions of the lower classes all contribute to the maintenance of an image of the masses which is marked by virulent hostility and animosity. We shall ask in this chapter whether or not this view is prevalent among the leaders studied, and how it is related to the set of ideas and characteristics which support belief in progress. Finally, is the image of the threatening masses verified by the facts; is it myth or reality?

Whether founded on myth or reality, the image of the hostile masses can be real in its consequences. Just as pessimism and the doubtful image of the future can facilitate the failures they anticipate, so also the belief that the lower classes are hostile may motivate or engender a style of behavior on the part of middle- and upper-class persons that could further estrange members of the lower classes. This may be particularly true if the view that the masses are hostile is held in official or quasi-official circles. Such an image of the masses may result in repressive legislation and action conducive to mass reaction, rather than more positive integrating measures. As one Jamaican columnist has observed:

> Already we spend four million pounds on internal security in the army and the police force. Much of it could be better spent on feeding people instead of preparing to shoot them when they become too hungry to care.[11]

Writing about the need for a change in thinking about the dissident groups in Jamaica, another journalist stated, "And if we think only in

---

[10] On more than one occasion my presence in some areas of West Kingston at odd hours was not too subtly probed by members of the security police. It is interesting to note that I was most often forewarned because their identity was quite well known in the area. Norris has suggested that persons showing an interest in the masses are liable to be suspected of being Communists. See Katrin Norris, *Jamaica: The Search for an Identity*, London: Oxford University Press for the Institute of Race Relations, 1962, p. 69.

[11] *Public Opinion*, XXVII (June 7, 1963), p. 13.

terms of repression, eventually we shall have a movement not far removed from the Mau Mau."[12]

As part of a discussion of the people and problems of West Kingston, the Jamaican leaders interviewed in this research were asked, "What would you say the people of West Kingston think of the middle- and upper-class people of Jamaica?" This question and the conversational probes that followed elicited detailed statements about the *typical* or *majority* view of the urban lower-class people. The content of these responses was analyzed to determine whether the leaders perceived the typical attitude to be one of hostility toward the more privileged classes in Jamaica. The leaders' perceptions of lower-class attitudes were:

The lower classes are hostile.	61%
They are not hostile.	39%
Total	100%
Number of cases	(51)
No answer	(3)

The majority of these leaders would have agreed with a nineteenth century West Indian colonial governor who wrote that he was ". . . convinced that the spirit of discontent is anything but extinct, it is alive as it were under its ashes,"[13] and with a recent writer: "So one might sum up all the information on Jamaica today: the island is littered with the remnants of a fire that is liable to flare up again. Jamaica is still branded by the institution of slavery."[14]

One question of immediate interest is whether the Jamaican leaders were correct in their assessment of the sentiments of the urban lower classes. Were the majority of the urban lower-class people hostile toward the middle and upper classes of Jamaica as 61 per cent of the leaders believed them to be? The findings of the survey in the selected urban lower-class area of Kingston clearly suggest the mythical nature of the leaders' image of the hostile masses. The attitudes toward the privileged classes actually expressed in interviews with the urban lower-class respondents were:[15]

---

[12] *Public Opinion*, XXVII (May 11, 1963), p. 2.
[13] Quoted in Ruth Glass, "Ashes of Discontent: The Past as Present in Jamaica," *Monthly Review*, XIV (May, 1962), p. 24.
[14] *Ibid.*
[15] Because one might expect reticence of lower-class respondents to express hostility, it should be noted that in analyzing the responses, any indication of hostility by indirect statement or even mode of expression was classified as a hostile response; also, the interviewing was done by two black or dark-skinned Jamaicans; see Appendix 1. It should be noted that 59 per cent of the lower-class respondents answering this question were women, and as might be expected they were some-

Hostility	20%
Indifference	12
Emulation	56
Friendship (mutual respect)	11
Mixed	1
Total	100%
Number of cases	120
No answer	(12)

One fifth of the lower-class respondents in West Kingston expressed hostility toward the middle and upper classes of Jamaica, whereas these sentiments of enmity and animosity were believed by 61 per cent of the leaders to be characteristic of the majority. The typical lower-class attitude was found to be one of emulation or aspiration to the standards of life and behavior exhibited by the privileged classes. As Henriques has said, commenting on the relations between segments of Jamaican society, ". . . the majority of the people, are constantly striving by every means in their power to emulate and imitate the European."[16] Indeed, more than half of the lower-class respondents indicated this desire to emulate the practices of the privileged classes. Only 11 per cent of the leaders reported such an attitude to be typical of the people of West Kingston.

Although one might wonder how widely accepted this mythical hostility of the lower classes is among the more socially distant middle- and upper-class population, the question of overriding significance turns upon the need to explain the leaders' remarkably inaccurate perceptions of the views of the people of West Kingston. It bears repeating in this context that all of these leaders were persons whose acknowledged social and civic responsibilities lie to some extent in West Kingston. All of them, because of their official positions or their public activities were more or less influential in the planning and implementation of policies directed to the solution of the problems of West Kingston and the people there. Yet, despite their concern and involvement with the area, the majority of these leaders asserted, apparently

---

what less likely to express hostility in the interviews than were the men. The phi correlation coefficient for the relationship between sex and expression of hostility was .22. A comparison of some interest may be made with a study of Africans' attitudes toward Europeans in Ghana before independence. Jahoda reported that two thirds of his sample of more than 200 adults were favorably inclined toward Europeans. See Gustav Jahoda, *White Man*, London: Oxford University Press, 1961, p. 58.

[16] Fernando Henriques, *Jamaica: Land of Wood and Water*, London: Macgibbon and Kee, 1957, p. 128.

incorrectly, that resentment and animosity were the dominant sentiments of the people. We should like to know why the majority of the leaders were mistaken in their acceptance of the myth of the hostile masses. What differentiated those leaders who perceived lower-class enmity and hostility from those who did not accept this view? And, importantly, how was the belief in progress related to this perceived antagonism of the masses?

The answer to this last question is presented in Table 27 where we may see the manner in which the perceived attitudes of the lower classes are reflected in the leaders' belief in progress. Forty-eight per

Table 27. PERCENTAGE OF JAMAICAN LEADERS WHO BELIEVE IN PROGRESS BY PERCEIVED ATTITUDES OF URBAN LOWER CLASS TOWARD THE UPPER AND MIDDLE CLASSES

Perceived Attitude of Urban Lower Classes	Percentage Who Believe in Progress	No. of Cases on Which the Per Cent is Based
Hostility	48	(31)
Non-hostility	60	(20)

cent of those leaders who saw the urban lower classes as hostile believed in progress compared to 60 per cent who did not perceive hostility as the typical response of the lower classes to the better-off segments of the society. This relationship between the perceptions of lower-class hostility and belief in progress may be further specified by reference to the social characteristics of the leaders. It was found that the original correlation was stronger for the older, the more highly educated, the brown-skinned, the higher occupational group, and those who were not aligned with the PNP. There was a less clear relationship between perception of lower-class hostility and belief in progress for the youngest leaders, the less educated, the white and black skinned leaders, and those with a low occupational rating. There was no relationship among those who preferred the Peoples' National Party. Perhaps the leaders whose status was more established or those who had more to lose were those whose views of Jamaica's potential were most affected by the perception of lower class hostility.

But before making such inferences we should examine the rest of the data. The correlation between the perception of hostility and belief in progress suggests the importance of the major variables, already introduced, which predicted the leaders' view of the future: the ideology of egalitarianism, the relative power of the leaders, and the knowledge of the discontents of the urban lower classes. What of their association with the perception of lower class hostility toward the more privileged classes of Jamaican society?

The role of the ideology of egalitarianism would not be unanticipated in its effect upon the perception of lower-class hostility. A person's views of his society are conditioned to some extent by the ideas and attitudes to which he subscribes. "That is to say, men have various ideological or judgmental views of different parts of their society, and these views may give them a 'false' or 'distorted' picture of their social world."[17] So among these leaders it was found that their attitudes toward equality induced selective perception of the views of the urban lower classes.[18] This is shown in Table 28 which presents the per-

Table 28. PERCENTAGE OF JAMAICAN LEADERS WHO PERCEIVE THE URBAN LOWER CLASSES TO BE HOSTILE BY EGALITARIANISM

Egalitarianism	Percentage Who Perceive Hostility	No. of Cases on Which the Per Cent is Based
Egalitarian	52	(29)
Inegalitarian	75	(20)

centage of Jamaican leaders who perceived urban lower-class hostility by egalitarianism. About half of the egalitarian leaders perceived hostility compared to three-quarters of the inegalitarians. Those leaders who favored the incorporation of all social, economic, and racial groups into meaningful participation in Jamaican society were not as likely to view the lower classes as hostile compared to those leaders who did not assert the importance of extending equality to all Jamaicans.

Examination of the second major variable reveals that leaders who were relatively less powerful were more often convinced of the hostility of the people of West Kingston than those leaders who scored high on the Index of Power. The percentage of leaders who perceived urban lower-class hostility by the Index of Power is presented in Table 29. Sixty-eight per cent of those leaders who received low scores on the Index of Power accepted the stereotype of the masses as hostile toward the more privileged classes. Among the more powerful leaders, 56 per

---

[17] Bernard Barber, *Social Stratification*, New York: Harcourt, Brace and Company, 1957, p. 187.
[18] For a somewhat comparable finding see Donald R. Matthews and James W. Prothro, "Southern Racial Attitudes: Conflict, Awareness, and Political Change," *The Annals of the American Academy of Political and Social Science*, 344 (November, 1962), pp. 108–121.

Table 29. PERCENTAGE OF JAMAICAN LEADERS WHO PERCEIVE THE URBAN LOWER CLASSES TO BE HOSTILE BY THE INDEX OF POWER

Index of Power	Percentage Who Perceive Hostility	No. of Cases on Which the Per Cent is Based
Most powerful	56	(25)
Least powerful	68	(25)

cent expressed the belief that the people of West Kingston were hostile toward those who had received more of the benefits of Jamaica's growth and development.

The lack of effective power may lead to a preoccupation with the lower classes as a threat to the stability and order which is often defined as a prerequisite to economic development. It may lead to blaming the lower classes for their own misfortunes. In this view, it is their unreasonable demands, their values, their expectations, their cries for "more, more," that are all in conflict with goals and values of the dominant minority who are trying to create the basis for a stable society; it is the masses who make it difficult to solve the problems Jamaica is facing; it is the masses who *are* the problem Jamaica is facing. This view would not be so easily accepted by those who have effective power. More powerful leaders are less likely to see the lower classes as hostile and as an insurmountable obstacle which destroys Jamaica's potential for future progress than less powerful leaders.

The leaders' scores on the Index of Knowledge also were related to the perception of hostility as the typical attitude of the lower classes. Those leaders with the least knowledge of the discontents of the urban lower classes were also most likely to perceive hostility. This sizeable difference in the perception of hostility by the Index of Knowledge is shown in Table 30. There we see that less than half of the knowledgeable leaders accepted the stereotyped hostility of the lower classes, while 85 per cent of the leaders with little knowledge expressed the conviction

Table 30. PERCENTAGE OF JAMAICAN LEADERS WHO PERCEIVE THE URBAN LOWER CLASSES TO BE HOSTILE BY THE INDEX OF KNOWLEDGE

Index of Knowledge	Percentage Who Perceive Hostility	No. of Cases on Which the Per Cent is Based
Most knowledgeable	45	(31)
Least knowledgeable	85	(20)

that the people of West Kingston were hostile toward the middle and upper classes. Hence, the imperfect patterns of communication which were inferred from the Index of Knowledge in the discussion of belief in progress are again found to influence the outlook of the leaders.[19] This finding would also tend to confirm suspicions that widespread enmity of the lower classes is indeed mythical.

We have seen that each of three variables, egalitarianism, the leaders' relative power in public affairs in West Kingston, and their knowledge of the problems of the people of the area was correlated with the differential perception of lower-class attitudes. We should now simultaneously examine the effect of all three variables upon the perception of lower-class hostility. Unfortunately, the small number of cases on which the analysis is based prohibits the presentation of the four-variable table. Therefore, the composite index of the three variables presented earlier will be used here also.[20] Those leaders who were egalitarian, powerful, and knowledgeable, were given scores of 3 on the composite index, while at the other extreme the inegalitarian, low-knowledge, and powerless leaders received a score of zero.

The percentage of leaders who perceived hostility as typical of the urban lower classes is presented by this composite index in Table 31.[21] Thirty per cent of the leaders who were egalitarian, most powerful, and

Table 31. **PERCENTAGE OF JAMAICAN LEADERS WHO PERCEIVE THE URBAN LOWER CLASSES TO BE HOSTILE BY THE COMPOSITE INDEX OF EGALITARIANISM, POWER AND KNOWLEDGE**

Composite Index Scores	Percentage Who Perceive Hostility	No. of Cases on Which the Per Cent is Based
3 (Highest)	30	(10)
2	62	(21)
0–1 (Lowest)	83	(18)

most knowledgeable (score 3) expressed the belief that the people of West Kingston were hostile to the privileged classes. At the other extreme, 83 per cent of those leaders who were assigned scores of zero

[19] This imperfect communication across class (and color) lines was found in the southern United States as well; *ibid.*
[20] This index was discussed in Chapter VII, *supra*.
[21] The zero and one scores were combined in Table 31 because of the small number of cases in the low scored cells of the table. In this case the table is isotropic and therefore the collapsing of categories does not obscure any reversal of the expected relationships, but it does somewhat obscure the high predictive efficiency of the composite index.

or one on the composite index perceived the lower class to be hostile. Sixty-two per cent of the leaders receiving a score of 2 perceived hostility among the masses.

The predictive efficiency of the composite index is somewhat obscured by the combination of the zero and one scores. The percentage of leaders perceiving hostility increases monotonically from 30 per cent for score 3 to 100 per cent for score zero. All of the inegalitarian, least powerful, and least knowledgeable leaders expressed the view that the masses were hostile toward the middle and upper classes. This finding is reduced to 83 per cent by the combination of scores called for by the small number of cases on which those percentages are based. Even so, there is a large difference between the extremes.

We have seen that the same three-variable configuration which served to predict belief in progress was an even better predictor of the leaders' perceived attitudes of the people of West Kingston. The contribution of the Index of Knowledge to the variation of leaders' perceptions of lower-class attitudes was particularly clear. As I mentioned before, this finding points up the mythical nature of the belief that the lower classes are typically hostile toward the privileged classes in Jamaica.

In the context of this discussion of inaccurate beliefs about attitudes and ideologies of Jamaican lower-class people, it is relevant to introduce some additional information from the survey carried out in Kingston, concerning the relationship between the acceptance of the idea of progress by lower-class people and variations in their level of political involvement. It became quite clear during the interviews with the leaders that the increasing size and density of the relatively low-income residential areas have become a source of growing concern as pockets of dissatisfaction and hostility. This attitude among Jamaican leaders is probably common to many leaders in other new and developing nations facing similar problems. The people who live in these economically depressed areas are frequently thought to be the least productive, least imaginative, most resentful, and a politically alienated group, whose ambitions are greatly limited by their fatalistic view of the world. In the foregoing discussion we have seen the largely mythical character of this alleged hostility, and, earlier, we have discussed the images of the past and future held by the lower classes. In addition to underscoring the fact that urban lower-class Jamaicans are not generally hostile, and that they have not uniformly rejected the possibility of progress, their acceptance of the idea of progress was positively associated with the extent of their mobilization into the political system of the island.

Political mobilization is used here to mean the ability to translate desires, complaints, and discontents into political terms as demands made upon the political system.[22] In order to use politics and political channels as a means for achieving their desires and satisfying their demands, people must have political contacts, they must know of persons or organizations who can meaningfully present their petitions to the political system, and they must perceive that their actions have some meaning in the political process. To allow an examination of the relationship between this involvement in the political process and the acceptance of the belief in progress among the lower-class Jamaicans studied, an Index of Political Mobilization was constructed based on data concerning their political contacts, their feelings of political efficacy, and their voting behavior. Summarized most simply, people who are aware of political agents they can contact, people who feel that they can be politically effective, and people who participate in politics at least by voting, are politically mobilized.[23] Scores on this measure of political mobilization ranged from zero to five with a mean score of 2.7.

It will be remembered from our earlier discussion that the respondents were asked to evaluate the trends of change in the past and to speculate about the future. For this analysis, those persons who both negatively evaluated the past trend of change in Jamaica and reported grim expectations for the future were classified as rejecting the idea of progress. About one third of the respondents were classified in this manner as persons who thought things had been going badly for Jamaica and were likely to continue to do so. Conversely, about two thirds of these lower-class respondents indicated that things were going well, that the trend of change was favorable, and that progress was likely. In Table 32, the percentage of these lower-class respondents who indicated a belief in progress is presented by levels of political mobilization. The distribution of percentages of respondents who believe in progress, with one minor reversal, decreases monotonically from a high of 92 per cent of those who are highly mobilized to a low of 38 per cent of those who are not mobilized. Simply stated, those in the West Kingston sample who were highly mobilized politically

---

[22] This definition follows that used by Linda Mirin and Arthur Stinchcombe in "The Political Mobilization of Mexican Peasants," presented at the meetings of the American Sociological Association, Montreal, Canada, September, 1964. This conception derives originally from Karl Deutsch, *Nationalism and Social Communication*, Cambridge, Mass.: The Technology Press of M.I.T. and New York: John Wiley and Sons, Inc., 1953, pp. 99–101.

[23] This measure of political mobilization is based on responses to the following items: whether the respondent knew of persons or organzations to whom he could voice his desires and complaints; whether he voted in the last election and referendum; and three political efficacy items concerning his perceptions of politicians, government officials, and the importance of voting.

Table 32. **PERCENTAGE OF URBAN LOWER-CLASS RESPONDENTS WHO BELIEVE IN PROGRESS BY LEVEL OF POLITICAL MOBILIZATION**

Political Mobilization Scores	Per Cent Believing in Progress	No. of Cases
5 (high)	92	(13)
4	82	(22)
3	72	(39)
2	50	(24)
1	38	(13)
0 (low)	41	(12)
	Total	(123)
	No answer	(9)

were more likely to believe in progress than those who were low on the measure of mobilization into the political system.

It appears from these data that the lack of understanding of politics on the part of many people who are not involved in the political process and the apparently incomprehensible actions of politicians who seem whimsical and capricious may promote a denial of the possibility of progress and an acceptance of fatalism.[24] The acceptance of the idea of progress among these lower-class Jamaicans seems to be based at least in part on their feelings of political efficacy, their involvement in the political system, and the perception of politics as within the reach of people like themselves.

In general, the findings reported in this chapter serve to emphasize that the urban lower-class Jamaicans studied are not generally hostile, nor are they uniformly fatalistic. Moreover, those persons who accept the idea of progress for Jamaica tend to be more strongly integrated into the political process by which their desired future might become fact than are those persons who view past and future trends of change in Jamaica as unfavorable. In addition, the sentiments of hostility believed by the majority of the Jamaican leaders to be typical of the urban lower classes toward the privileged classes of Jamaica are not borne out by the attitudes actually expressed by a sample of lower-class persons in West Kingston. Whereas 61 per cent of the leaders reported the majority of the lower-class persons to be hostile, in fact 20 per cent of the lower-class persons interviewed indicated such hostile attitudes. Further, those leaders who by their attitudes toward equality indicated a preference for maximizing the breadth and intensity of social

---

[24] This interpretation is suggested by David Riesman and Nathan Glazer in "Criteria for Political Apathy," in Alvin W. Gouldner (ed.), *Studies in Leadership*, New York: Harper and Brothers, 1950, p. 525. It is empirically supported by Mirin and Stinchcombe in their study of political mobilization among Mexican peasants, *op. cit.*, p. 10.

relations among all Jamaicans and who were also more knowledgeable and capable of exerting greater social pressure in public affairs of West Kingston were most likely to reject the myth of the hostile masses as an unrealistic view of the relations between classes in Jamaica. Those leaders, who by preference or circumstances were limited in their involvement with West Kingston, were most likely to perceive inaccurately the sentiments of the urban lower classes toward the privileged classes. The majority of the leaders seem to confirm one of Eric Hoffer's many aphorisms. He wrote, "There is a tendency to judge a race, a nation or any distinct group by its least worthy members."[25] The myth of the hostile masses in Jamaica would seem to be based on just such a tendency. There can be no denial that one encounters hostility among the people of West Kingston. This is particularly true of some members of the Ras Tafari cult and others who don their symbols. Overt manifestations of hostile attitudes are more likely to be highly visible than those of indifference, friendship, or the desire to emulate others. Hostility gains attention more readily because of its association with threats to one's security. Reports of "incidents" and violent expressions of illiterate resentment rapidly gain in significance and detail with the momentum of rumor and exaggeration. To focus attention on these incidents is to foster an incomplete conception of the views of the people of West Kingston toward the privileged segments of Jamaican society. From the data reported here one must insist that *hostility is far from the typical response of lower-class people to the better-off segments of Jamaican society.*

The implications of the leaders' inaccurate views and the consequences of the behavior they might engender are fearsome. Some of the implications of the belief that the masses represent a threat were suggested by the disproportionately strong reaction to the Coral Gardens "uprising" in April, 1963. Another hint of this tendency to resort to repressive action was given only a few days prior to the Coral Gardens incident. The Unemployed Workers' Council had planned a march and demonstration in Kingston on March 31, 1963. The government's immediate reaction was a display of force with the intention of intimidating the dissenters. The march was banned and "armored cars rumbled through the streets of Kingston," in Jamaica's version of what used to be called "gunboat diplomacy."[26] The significance of such action in the face of any opposition demonstration lies in the threat to democratic processes, and in the kind of behavior it may generate in return. In these few instances the stage has been set for the vicious

---

[25] Eric Hoffer, *The True Believer*, New York: New American Library, 1951, p. 29.
[26] *Spotlight*, Kingston, Jamaica, XXIV (March, 1963), p. 10.

circle of the self-fulfilling prophecy in which ill-founded fears give rise to their own spurious confirmation.[27] The belief that the lower classes in Jamaica are hostile may be conducive to a style of behavior on the part of the government and the middle- and upper-class people which could give truth to the initially false definition of the situation.

Although this false definition of the sentiments of the urban lower-class people could clearly assume the character of a self-fulfilling prophecy, the findings reported here also suggest that the fatalistic prophecy might not, and certainly need not, be fulfilled. Obviously, there is discontent among the people of West Kingston, but it need not result in widespread hostility and overt aggression unless these are provoked by unenlightened leadership. The prophecy might not be fulfilled because the knowledgeable and powerful leaders, guided by their commitment to the ideology of equality, reject the myth of the hostile masses. If these leaders do not deny their ideology and their responsibility, "the tragic circle of fear, social disaster, and reinforced fear can be broken."[28]

---

[27] Robert K. Merton, "The Self-fulfilling Prophecy," *Social Theory and Social Structure*, (rev. ed.) Glencoe, Ill.: The Free Press, 1957, pp. 421–436.
[28] *Ibid.*, p. 436.

CHAPTER 9 Conclusion

In Jamaica as in many other emerging countries, new national leaders have recently gained control of their country's future history. Numerous aspects of social, economic, and political change are becoming the objects of history-making decisions. The new leaders' images of the future, their attitudes toward change, their time perspectives, and their expectations regarding the nation's potential have become critically important to the process of nation-building. As Lucian Pye has observed, nation-building requires a sense of predictability which "... can widen a people's belief in the range of possible eventualities; it can provide them with a greater sense of command over their fate; and it can encourage them to raise their levels of collective ambition."[1] The role of expectancy is a powerful one. Expectations concerning the range of possible futures are critically important elements in the decision-making which will shape a new nation's history.

The research reported here is a study of the images of the future held by public leaders. Jamaican leaders' attitudes toward the progressive development of their nation's potential, specifically, their beliefs in progress, were analyzed in relation to their commitments to the ideal of equality, their relative power in public affairs, and their knowledge of the discontents of the urban lower-class people whose welfare was their responsibility. These three major attributes of the leaders were also utilized in the analysis of their stereotypes of the urban lower classes.

The close link between the ideals of equality and progress which emerged from the democratic revolution of the eighteenth century was evident among the attitudes of Jamaican leaders. Those leaders who favored the extension of equality of opportunity to all persons, and opposed the maintenance of ascriptive barriers to full participation in Jamaican society, were likely to believe in progress. The leaders not clearly favoring the reduction of such barriers to participation in the

---

[1] Lucian W. Pye, *Politics, Personality, and Nation Building: Burma's Search for Identity*, New Haven: Yale University Press, 1962, p. 293.

society, economy, and polity were not likely to believe in the progressive character of Jamaica's developing potential. Thus, for most of these leaders, the belief in progress was associated with desired changes in Jamaica's social structure, particularly the incorporation of the less privileged social, economic, and racial segments of the population into equal and meaningful participation in the nation's future. On the whole, the Enlightenment tradition of thought and its influence throughout Western civilization may be seen among these Jamaican leaders. Of the majority who affirmed the value of equality, most were believers in progress.

The command of some measure of control in the movement toward the future, the possession of access to the means of decisions which affect the future of the nation, also contributed to the frequency of belief in progress. In expressing their images of the future, those leaders who were relatively more powerful most often indicated their faith in the favorability of Jamaica's coming history. The less powerful leaders most often negated the possibility of Jamaica's potential for progress.

This analysis of the effect of the leaders' relative power upon their attitudes toward progress was elaborated by the introduction of their views regarding the ideal of equality. It was found that both power and egalitarianism contributed independently to the prediction of attitudes toward progress. Irrespective of their relative power, the egalitarian leaders most frequently believed in progress, and when the effects of attitudes toward equality were controlled, the most powerful leaders were likely to hold favorable views of the island's developing future. Generally, those leaders who had access to the means of history-making decisions and who expressed commitment to egalitarianism were more likely to believe in progress than inegalitarian and less powerful leaders.

Knowledge, in addition to power and egalitarianism, is a critically important component in the process of making the decisions that shape the future. Further, it was contended, following Boulding,[2] that it is through knowledge that we can hope to control society and fulfill the positive images of the future. In this context, the association between knowledge and belief in future progress was examined. Knowledge was found to play an important role in the leaders' belief in progress. Those leaders who were most knowledgeable about the urban lower classes were likely to hold favorable views of Jamaica's potential. The less knowledgeable leaders did not as frequently express faith in the progressive future for their island-nation. This finding suggests that belief in progress was not to be lightly dismissed as the expression of

---

[2] Kenneth Boulding, "Relations of Economic, Political and Social Systems," *Social and Economic Studies*, XI (December, 1962), p. 358.

Lower-class neighborhoods of West Kingston. *(Photographs by John W. Evans)*. See also following pages.

A West Kingston man in front of his house. (*Courtesy of Jamaica Information Service*).

Norman W. Manley, as premier, visited with a group of Rastafarians in West Kingston. (*Gleaner Photo*).

A pocomania religious leader of the sort popular in West Kingston. (*Courtesy of Jamaica Tourist Board*).

Some old and some new government housing units. *(Photographs by John W. Evans).*

an unrealistic and unknowing idealism. The more pessimistic view of the future, which some people might be tempted to call "realism," was founded on ignorance.

Each of these three major variables, egalitarianism, power, and knowledge was found to predict an additional portion of the variation in attitudes toward progress. In sum, those leaders who were egalitarian, powerful, and knowledgeable, were more likely to believe in progress than those who did not favor equality, were less powerful, and less knowledgeable about the discontents of the lower-class people.

Finally, it was shown that the same three-variable configuration which served to predict the leaders' attitudes toward progress was an even better predictor of their stereotypical thinking about the lower classes. Egalitarian, powerful and knowledgeable leaders were most likely to reject the myth of the hostile masses as an unrealistic view of the relations between classes in Jamaica. Comparisons of the leaders' perceptions of hostility with the frequency of expressions of hostility by the sample of urban lower-class people seemed to confirm the mythical nature of the stereotype of the threatening masses.

With respect to the role of knowledge in belief in progress, it was suggested that it may be awareness of the lower-class people as a resource to be mobilized and developed that supported the favorable view of the future of West Kingston and Jamaica. This same awareness of the positive, rather than the negative and undesirable, character of the lower classes may well explain the rejection of the belief that the masses are hostile to the privileged classes, and are thereby an obstacle to Jamaica's development rather than a contributor to it.

Some implications of the belief that the masses are a threat to the stability of the nation's future were suggested by the disproportionately strong and repressive reaction to the "uprising" in April, 1963. Given the findings reported here, on the myth of the hostile masses, it would be unfortunate if the Government needlessly devoted their energies and resources to the development of agencies and instruments of repression rather than to maximize the potential for reform and progression.

In the period since this research was completed a great many things have happened in Jamaica, too many to be cataloged here, but not much has really changed. Economic growth appears to have increased again after levelling off in the first two years after independence, but the critical problems of the distribution of the benefits of this growth, including the provision of more jobs, remain largely untouched. Increasing unemployment is behind nearly every pressing problem facing the island-nation. Jamaica's most abundant resource is its people, and they are poorly utilized and not being mobilized and practically equipped for the move into a better future for themselves and the nation. This was true five years ago and it is equally true now. Much has happened in these years; not much has changed. The changes that one can point to, such as the establishment of a National Insurance scheme for the provision of social security benefits, the building of low cost housing schemes, the opening of new harbor facilities, the inauguration of new agricultural programs, and many others, have done essentially nothing toward resolving the major problems of the widening gap between the majority of poor Jamaicans and the rest. A second major cleavage that divides the population is the strong political sentiment that is based heavily on the charismatic natures of the waning leaders, Bustamante and Manley. This political division of the nation since long before independence has allowed the various governments to temporize when faced with the need to provide at least minimum economic rights for all. It is possible that this could continue for a long while, but it does not seem likely. Bolder new thinking and more radical proposals are beginning to come from many of the new younger nationalist leaders who are committed to an ethic of equality, and who are moving into positions of power convinced that their nation's future can be better than was possible under colonial rule.

Our findings also result in a favorable view of Jamaica's new history. More than half of the leaders studied expressed belief in Jamaica's future potential for progressive change. The believers in progress tended to be persons who were in a position to exert some control in the councils of decision which will shape the nation's future. They tended to be knowledgeable people who will be guided in their history-making decisions by commitments to the ideal of equality. If the assumptions made here are well founded, we shall see the past and present trends of progressive change continue, and even be accelerated by the support of more and more members of Jamaican society. But even belief in the idea of progress can be a damning kind of fatalism, if it becomes a faith that fosters inaction and a negation of the normative implications of the idea of progress. Or, if the leaders who are capable of influencing the trends of change abdicate their responsibility and shed their ideology for reasons of self-interest or despair, then those progressive trends may falter.

Perhaps we have seen some tendency toward this latter situation already in Jamaica. I speak of some of the leaders who were aligned with the PNP, the former governing party of Jamaica. In general, they were egalitarian, highly knowledgeable, and half of them were classified as relatively powerful. Yet, as a group, those who preferred the PNP were the least likely to believe in progress. These persons who had defined themselves as leaders of change, founders of the nationalist movement for self-government and a political party in the

Fabian tradition, had in a few months' time, seen their federationist policy rejected, and most importantly their national plan and achievements denied at the polls. Their failure to believe in progress may well be due to these disappointing blows. But, their almost defeatist attitudes, and the fatalist images of the future held by these and other leaders, may have unfortunate consequences if they induce a style of behavior, a character of policy, or a negation of responsibility which is inimical to the maintenance of the current progressive trends. What is desirable rather than disillusionment and false despair is, in the words of Heilbroner, ". . . a point of view which sees in the juggernaut of history's forces both the means by which progress painfully made in the past may be trampled underfoot, and the means by which a broader and stronger base for progress in the future may be brought into being."[3]

[3] Robert L. Heilbroner, *The Future as History,* New York: Grove Press, Inc., 1961, p. 208.

APPENDIX 1 Field Work and Study Design

The data reported here were collected in Jamaica between August 7, 1961, and September 21, 1962. These thirteen months were marked by three highly significant events for Jamaica. Growing anti-federation sentiment culminated in a referendum to determine whether Jamaica would remain in the West Indies Federation. This referendum, on September 19, 1961 resulted in Jamaica's withdrawal from the federal union and the Federation's eventual collapse. Jamaicans had decided to go into independence as a separate nation. On the heels of this decision came the call for general elections to determine which political party would form the first government of the new nation. These elections, on April 10, 1962, brought victory to the Jamaica Labour Party and a new government in independence. Finally, political independence was granted to Jamaica on August 6, 1962, when the island-nation became a Dominion in the British Commonwealth and the first new nation in the Western hemisphere in this century. These three events, the referendum decision to "go it alone," the general elections resulting in a new government, and the advent of political independence, along with the campaigns and preparations which accompanied them, served to enhance the richness and significance of the data collected during that period. It is hard to imagine a single year filled with more changes of such importance to the people of Jamaica than 1961–1962. One could hardly have wished for a better time to study attitudes toward the trend of change, past, present, and particularly future, than when the people were so aware of, so often thinking about, and so willing to talk about Jamaica's future. For, as independence approached, the Jamaican citizenry were preoccupied with speculations about the island's potential, its problems, and the likelihood of making independence a success.

The elections and the coming independence resulted in many replacements among the politicians and appointed officials who were relevant to the subject of this research. These changes, and the emotional aftermath of the elections among the mass of average Jamaicans, led to the postponement of formal data collection until May, 1962.

Meanwhile, preparatory research was in progress and the formal study was being planned. Preliminary interviews were conducted with policy-makers, politicians, civil servants, and other officials in both governmental and non-governmental agencies. These interviews were not intended to collect the basic data of the study, but to yield information which would aid in the final formulation of the research problem and in the specification of the research design. They also served importantly to familiarize me with the research situation and to help develop a nucleus of informants which I maintained during my entire stay in Jamaica.

These preliminary interviews were instrumental in the delineation of a manageable unit of analysis which involved limited, yet significant obstacles facing independent Jamaica. The research called for a problem or issue about which there was some ongoing discussion so that potential respondents would have given it some thought. Preliminary interviewing revealed that among the numerous nationally significant problems during this period of change, one that was uppermost as a source of concern and controversy among policy-makers and intellectuals centered around the people of West Kingston, the growing urban lower classes. West Kingston had become an urban "reception center" for the growing numbers of migrants from the rural areas,[1] and was viewed by many Jamaicans as a symbol of the shortcomings of a development program which was creating new problems while overcoming others.

In addition, the problems symbolized by West Kingston were a relatively manageable and significant issue. This focus consolidated a social issue, a geographical area, and social, economic, and political problems that linked it significantly with the development of the island as a whole. Moreover, when one asked someone about the area and its people, he knew what was being referred to, and would usually have some definite opinions. These views were often pre-judgments or took the form of a harangue based on ignorance, but, whether well informed or not, most people had some opinion on the subject of what should be done for the people or *to* the people of West Kingston.

[1] This may be shown briefly by consideration of the 1960 census. While the population of the island increased by 30 per cent since the 1943 census, the population of the Kingston Metropolitan area increased by 87 per cent. Even more striking was the increase of 173.6 per cent since 1943 in urban St. Andrew. A large part of the area broadly referred to here as "West Kingston" falls within that district. See the *Economic Survey 1960*, and *Economic Survey 1961*, published by the government of Jamaica; see also the discussion of migration to West Kingston in George Eaton Simpson, "Jamaican Revivalist Cults," *Social and Economic Studies*, V (December, 1956), pp. 322–323; and G. E. Cumper, "Population Movements in Jamaica," *Social and Economic Studies*, V (September, 1956), p. 272.

These preliminary interviews were done in a non-random and snowball manner with each person being asked who else he thought I should be interested in seeing. Usually I described my research interests very broadly and focused discussion on the problems of social change and development of Jamaica as a nation. As I have mentioned, these discussions frequently referred to the growing urban lower classes and the resulting difficulties for Jamaica's successful social and economic development. This focus emerged early as a topic of prime concern. The content of these interviews served to define the subject matter of the research and to inform my thought and reading in the preparation of the research design and interview schedules.

The trial of different strategies of research method and technique was also possible in these preparatory interviews. For example, it was after having tried some forced-choice questions in this setting that I decided to reject that technique in favor of probing open-ended questions which seemed more congenial to the leaders because of the conversational manner in which they could be asked. Although the forced-choice approach would have left less room for equivocation on the part of the respondent (and the interviewer), it seemed that most of the persons felt uncomfortably constrained by the necessity of making such choices. Several of my informants with whom I often tried out questions also supported this decision.

Another important, however less systematic, source of observations was provided by the many public street meetings held during the election campaign. Such meetings are one of the major forms of political communication in Jamaica. I attended two or three of these meetings per night, almost every night, from the time the elections were announced in February until the eve of polling day in April. Travelling from one meeting to another, most frequently in the urban lower-class constituencies on the West Side, I soon realized that the content of the campaign oratory varied little from one party to another, from one candidate to another, or from one section of the area to another. Each party spoke glowingly of its "Man with the Plan," or "The Party with the Program," but the focus on issues was minimal. The racist appeals of the newly formed, African-oriented, Peoples' Political Party were only more blatant than those issuing from other platforms on the West Side. The importance of attending these meetings came not from the speeches, but from talking with the listeners. These informal associations, some of which continued in the months after the election, were an important source of information for this research. Frequently, the midnight hours after these meetings would be spent in serious and excited political discussion in some yard in Greenwich Town, Trench Town, Cockburn Pen, or one of the other sections of West Kingston.

These sessions provided much of the elaboration of the context within which I came to view the research. For instance, the myth of a generalized lower-class hostility became even more clearly mythical, and more clearly important as an attitude held by many Jamaicans who perhaps ought to have known better. These contacts also informed the attempts to construct an adequate interview schedule for the Trench Town survey which was to begin only a few weeks later.[2]

Although I must emphasize that these informal associations with the lower-class people and with politicians and government officers were not a source of systematically collected data, it is equally true that the informal talks and the preliminary interviews were an important part of the research operation that served as a foundation for the data reported here. The significance assigned to various findings, and often the manner in which they have been interpreted, has undoubtedly been influenced by these more impressionistic insights based on "participant" observation.[3]

A final comment concerning the utility of this approach in the fieldwork concerns the problem of adequate communication and understanding. As most newcomers to Jamaica will readily agree, the variants of English which are spoken make much of the lower-class speech unintelligible to the outsider. For example, a study of social stratification in a Jamaican market town excluded the lower classes because of this difficulty.[4] This language difference also exists for the middle- and upper-class Jamaicans. Smith reports that these people do not understand 30 per cent of the words of the folk dialect.[5] By means of these informal meetings and the cultivation of several informants among the lower classes I was able to overcome this difficulty to some extent. This was, of course, important in carrying out the Trench Town sample survey.

STUDY DESIGN

The details of research method for the two sources of data are discussed separately. The study of Jamaican leaders was based on a

---

[2] The skeptic will immediately suggest, as many Jamaican middle-class people did, that these lower-class persons were willing to talk with me only to set me up as a target for exploitation. To a minor extent this was true during my early experience, but as I became more known in the area, and learned the proper behavior, such confrontations were less and less frequent.

[3] I have enclosed participant in quotation marks because as an obvious outsider, I could only be a participant in a limited sense.

[4] Robert A. Ellis, "Color and Class in a Jamaican Market Town," *Sociology and Social Research*, XLI (May–June, 1957), pp. 354–360.

[5] M. G. Smith, "The Plural Framework of Jamaican Society," *The British Journal of Sociology*, XII (September, 1961), p. 259.

different methodology and was faced with different problems than the lower-class inquiry. In addition, the lower-class survey data are drawn from a larger study, only a small part of which is reported here.

The study of Jamaican leaders. When the prospect of studying Jamaican leaders arose, the first problem was the definition of the universe of leaders. "Leaders" were defined as persons who were influential in spheres of decision-making and the formulation and implementation of policy relevant to a given issue-area, West Kingston and the urban lower classes. The decision to use reputational methods, or the "power attribution" approach, provided the final basis for the definition of the universe of leaders to be studied. The major assumption involved in the choice of this approach was that those persons thought, by knowledgeable informants, to be influential in policy formation and implementation are more likely to be influential in those processes than those who do not have such a reputation. With this assumption in mind, the reputational approach was here used as a purposive sampling technique by which the universe of leaders under observation could be operationally defined. This is best explained by a description of the procedure followed.

The first person interviewed in the process of formal data collection, was chosen by both reputational and positional criteria. He was an elected politician of high standing and had been frequently mentioned in the preliminary interviews as a person whose views on West Kingston I should hear. He was asked:

> Now, I'd like you to tell me the names of the people you think are most important in determining and carrying out policy in relation to the problems of West Kingston.

From the listing of names provided by this respondent I then chose another leader, also a politician, who was both positionally and reputationally prominent in relation to West Kingston. This procedure was followed for the third interviewee also, but thereafter any person nominated by three or more respondents was included in the universe of leaders. By this method the universe of leaders grew to include 64 persons who had received the requisite three nominations. Two persons who had received less than three mentions were included in the final universe of potential respondents for good reasons. Both were elected politicians whose duties involved them in West Kingston. One was a newly appointed Member of Cabinet whose ministerial responsibility was directly relevant to the problems of West Kingston. His appointment was made after the interviewing was well along, and therefore he might have been included by the reputational criterion, as other Cabinet Ministers were, had his appointment preceded the beginning of the formal data collection. Rather than assume a static universe of leaders, I thought it best to include him (and any others had the situation occurred) on a positional basis, and thereby reflect the changes that actually took place. The other person included was selected also primarily on the basis of the position he held. He was a leading member of the opposition party, a Member of Parliament, and a national leader of long standing. In addition, two of my informants suggested that this person would probably not be mentioned because most respondents would certainly take for granted that I was aware of his importance. The latter reason alone is indeed feeble, but when viewed in conjunction with the positional criterion I think his inclusion is valid.

The inclusion of these two additional persons as leaders brought the universe to a total of 66 persons. Fifty-four leaders or 82 per cent of the potential respondents were interviewed. Interviews were completed with 90 per cent of the 50 top-ranked persons in the universe. While the 54 interviews constitute a sample of the universe of 66 persons, they are here treated as the universe for the purposes of analysis and discussion. Interviews could not be completed with five persons in the universe because they were temporarily off the island. I was unable to arrange appointments with the remaining seven persons for various reasons. None of these persons openly refused to see me, or said they would rather not be interviewed.

Before leaving this aspect of the methodology, the current criticisms of reputational methods should be considered briefly. Most critiques of reputational methods are directed at their use in the study of community power rather than as a means of drawing a purposive sample for investigations which are concerned with something other than a description of a power structure.[6] This research was not attempting

[6] The several critical points of view are found in Robert A. Dahl, "A Critique of the Ruling Elite Model," *American Political Science Review*, LII (June, 1958), pp. 463–469; Nelson W. Polsby, "The Sociology of Community Power: A Reassessment," *Social Forces*, XXXVII (March, 1959), pp. 233–236; Nelson W. Polsby, "Three Problems in the Analysis of Community Power," *American Sociological Review*, XXIV (December, 1959), pp. 796–803; Nelson W. Polsby, "Community Power: Some Reflections on the Recent Literature," *American Sociological Review*, XXVII (December, 1962), pp. 838–841; Raymond Wolfinger, "Reputation and Reality in the Study of 'Community Power,'" *American Sociological Review*, XXV (October, 1960), pp. 636–644; and Raymond Wolfinger, "A Plea for a Decent Burial," *American Sociological Review*, XXVII (December, 1962), pp. 841–847. For a rebuttal by the adherents of the reputational approach see William V. D'Antonio and Eugene C. Erickson, "The Reputational Technique as a Measure of Community Power: An Evaluation Based on Comparative and Longitudinal Studies," *American Sociological Review*, XXVII (June, 1962), pp. 362–376; William V. D'Antonio, Howard J. Erlich, and Eugene C. Erickson, "Further Notes on the Study of Community Power," *American Sociological Review*, XXVII (December, 1962), pp. 848–854.

Table A1. PERCENTAGE DISTRIBUTION OF JAMAICAN LEADERS ACCORDING TO SELECTED SOCIAL CHARACTERISTICS

Selected Characteristic	Jamaican Leaders (Per Cent)
Sex	
Men	89
Women	11
Total	100
Number of cases	(54)
Country of Birth	
Jamaica	88
Other	12
Total	100
Number of cases	(51)
No information	(3)
Age	
50 years or older	37
40–49 years	41
39 years or younger	22
Total	100
Number of cases	(54)
Race–Color	
White	26
Brown	26
Black	48
Total	100
Number of cases	(54)
Occupational Rating	
1 (Highest)	50
2–4 (Lowest)	50
Total	100
Number of cases	(54)
Religious Preference	
Anglican	38
Other Protestant	41
Roman Catholic	18
Jewish	3
Total	100
Number of cases	(39)
No information	(15)
Political Party Preference	
Jamaica Labour Party	24
Peoples' National Party	48
Other (no known preference)	28
Total	100
Number of cases	(54)

to describe the political system, nor to isolate a general power structure. It did not assume the existence of a monolithic ruling elite, nor that the distribution of power and influence was static. There was no *a priori* limitation set on the size of the universe; rather it was defined by the respondents themselves. Finally, the universe defined by this reputational method was delineated by reference to a specific issue in the context of Jamaica's development, rather than in terms of a generalized power structure.

Most of the interviews were conducted in the respondents' offices. One quarter took place in their homes. The average interview lasted one hour and twenty-five minutes with the longest running three hours and the shortest twenty-five minutes. The interview schedule is presented in Appendix 3.

The composition of the universe of leaders defined by the reputational technique is, of course, considerably different from that studied by Bell in his 1958 questionnaire study of elites.[7] It is also a somewhat different group than that studied by Moskos in his research on nationalism in 1962.[8] The social characteristics and type of elite positions of the leaders interviewed in this research are presented in Tables A1 and A2. These percentage distributions provide a summary description of the universe of leaders.

Table A2. PERCENTAGE DISTRIBUTION OF JAMAICAN LEADERS ACCORDING TO TYPE OF ELITE POSITION

Position	Jamaican Leaders (Per Cent)	
Elected Politicians		39
Members of Parliament	24	
Parish Councillors	15	
Government Officers		30
Civil Servants	19	
Jamaica Social Welfare Commission	11	
Non-Governmental Community Welfare Leaders		32
Clergy	17	
Other	15	
Total	100	100
Number of cases	(54)	(54)

The West Kingston survey. The data reported for the sample of West Kingston residents were collected in collaboration with Professor

[7] Wendell Bell, *Jamaican Leaders: Political Attitudes in a New Nation*, Berkeley and Los Angeles: University of California Press, 1964.
[8] Charles C. Moskos, Jr., *The Sociology of Political Independence: A Study of Nationalist Attitudes Among West Indian Leaders*, Cambridge, Mass.: Schenkman Publishing Co., 1967.

Walter E. Freeman, Michigan State University, and with the cooperation of the Urban Community Development Staff of the Jamaica Social Welfare Commission.

West Kingston, the issue-area on which the research focussed, was described in Chapter 2. The social area sampled, an extremely low income district occupied almost exclusively by squatters, was chosen because it represents what was thought to be the culmination of many of the shortcomings of Jamaica's development program. The area was a part of Trench Town into which the Jamaica Social Welfare Commission was planning to expand its urban community development work, but at the time the survey was completed they had not yet begun their work in that section.

A 25 per cent systematic random sample of households representing a total universe of 537 households was drawn. Specifically, the sampling was carried out while the interviewing was in process, with every fourth household included in the sample, the first house being chosen randomly. This method of household selection was followed at the beginning of each new block. Substitutions were made in the sample in five cases in which it was not possible to make contact with a suitable respondent in a chosen household. If call-backs were unsuccessful, the procedure for substitutions was simply to take the preceding and the following household alternately. There were 134 units in the sample, in which 132 usable interviews were completed. The average size of the households in the sample was 3.5 persons. If this average is applied to the known total of households, we see that the respondents were drawn from a population of approximately 1,880 persons.[9]

The persons interviewed were the "heads of households" chosen non-randomly within the household. A person was accepted as a head of a household if he (or she) lived in the house and contributed to the maintenance of the household. For example, an adult sister of the "home owner," who lived there and cared for the children of the family was accepted as a suitable respondent. Thus, many households had multiple heads.

All of the interviews were obtained between May 15, 1962 and July 11, 1962, with 96 per cent completed by June 17, 1962. The interviews were conducted in the yard or home of the respondents by two dark-skinned Jamaicans. In several cases the investigators participated in the interviews in order that we might be aware of the difficulties calling for modification of the interview schedule, and to have a better grasp of the nature of the interview situation and the responses.

[9] The area was enumerated by the Welfare Commission shortly before this research was conducted. Their figures were 529 households, 3.5 persons per household, and a total of 1,840 persons.

Pretest interviews were conducted as a trial of the wording of questions and organization of the interview schedule. In addition, minor modifications were made after 16 interviews had been completed. These changes in no way altered the meaning of any questions, but simply clarified some questions, and included suggested probe questions.

Two training sessions were held with each interviewer in preparation for the data collection. In addition, the interviewers observed each other, and the investigators in some initial interviews in order to illustrate different techniques of probing and helping the respondent to remember the information requested. After these interviews we then discussed any difficulties encountered and suggested ways they might be overcome.

Table A3. PERCENTAGE DISTRIBUTION OF URBAN LOWER-CLASS RESPONDENTS ACCORDING TO SELECTED SOCIAL CHARACTERISTICS

Selected Characteristic		Urban Lower-Class Respondents (Per Cent)
Age		
15–24 years		10
25–34		32
35–44		25
45–54		15
55–64		13
65 years and older		5
	Total	100
	Number of cases	(126)
	No information	(6)
Sex		
Men		38
Women		62
	Total	100
	Number of cases	(132)
Education		
Never attended school		7
Less than two years		16
2–4 years		33
5–6		43
7 or more years		1
	Total	100
	Number of cases	(127)
	No information	(5)
Employment Status		
Steadily employed		37
Occasionally employed		25
Unemployed		37
Registered pauper		1
	Total	100
	Number of cases	(132)

Table A3 (Continued)

Selected Characteristic	Urban Lower-Class Respondents (Per Cent)
Occupation	
Clerical	2
Commercial	31
Services	17
Skilled trades	7
Handicrafts	14
Factory worker	2
Transport worker	2
Laborer	17
Other	8
Total	100
Number of cases	(132)
Estimated Annual Income From Work	
Under £ 50	45
£ 50– £ 99	14
£100– £149	11
£150– £199	7
£200– £249	6
£250– £299	6
£300 or more	11
Total	100
Number of cases	(125)
No information	(7)
Marital Status	
Currently married	16
Not currently married	6
Never married	78
Total	100
Number of cases	(130)
No information	(2)
Number of Persons in Household	
Single person	10
2 persons	25
3–4	28
5–6	23
7–8	10
9 or more	4
Total	100
Number of cases	(132)
Political Party Preference	
None	24
Jamaica Labour Party	49
Peoples' National Party	25
Peoples' Political Party	2
Total	100
Number of cases	(128)
No information	(4)

The composition of the lower-class sample drawn in West Kingston (Trench Town) is summarized in Table A3. There, the percentage distribution of respondents is given according to selected social characteristics.

APPENDIX 2 Index Construction

This appendix contains the details of the Occupational Rating Scale, the Index of Power, and the Index of Knowledge which were used in the analysis of belief in progress.

Occupational ratings. The method of ranking leaders by their occupation was the same as that used by Wendell Bell in his 1958 study of Jamaican elites.[1] This system of occupational ratings was adapted by Bell for use in Jamaica from the work of Warner and his associates.[2] Information on occupations of the leaders collected by this writer was supplemented by the use of *Who's Who, Jamaica,* and *The Handbook of Jamaica.*[3]

In addition to the Table of Occupational Ratings presented below, the classification of leader's occupations was guided by the following specifications: (1) professional status was given precedence over "white collar" status when applicable; (2) barristers and solicitors with college education or other occupations were ranked "1," otherwise they were ranked "2"; (3) if civil servants' positions were not clearly classifiable by the scale then rank was determined by salary with over £1,650 ranked "1," £1,200 to £1,649 ranked "2," and less than £1,200 ranked "3."

The Index of Power. This index is more properly called an Index of Relative Power in Public Affairs relating to West Kingston. The Index has two components. The first is a score computed for each in-

---

[1] Wendell Bell, *Jamaican Leaders: Political Attitudes in a New Nation,* Berkeley and Los Angeles: University of California Press, 1964, Appendix I.

[2] Adapted by Bell from W. Lloyd Warner, Marchia Meeker, Kenneth Eells, *Social Class in America,* Chicago: Science Research Associates, Inc., 1949, pp. 140–141, and Carson McGuire, "Social Status, Peer Status, and Social Mobility," a mimeographed memorandum for research workers based upon procedures used in studies for the Committee on Human Development, University of Chicago, Chicago, Ill., 1948.

[3] *Who's Who, Jamaica 1960,* edited by Clifton Neita, Kingston, Jamaica: The Gleaner Co., Ltd., 1960; and *The Handbook of Jamaica for 1961,* Kingston, Jamaica: The Government Printing Office, 1961.

Table A4. OCCUPATIONAL RATINGS

Occupational Rating	Professionals	Proprietors
1 (Highest)	Doctor, dentist, engineer, judge, lawyer, clergyman, professor, school superintendent, headmaster of secondary school, architect, statistician, et al.	Investment of $75–100,000 in business or industry — varies by community size.
2	High school teacher, headmaster of elementary school, trained nurse (RN), chiropodist, chiropractor, mortician, clergyman (no college), engineer (no college), veterinary.	Reputed value of $20–70,000 — "a very good business, but not the largest kind."
3	Grade school teacher, optician, assistant to undertaker, city veterinary, employed pharmacist (any unionized profession), land surveyor.	Value or equity reputed $5–20,000 in a "good" but rather "small" business, etc.
4		Value or equity in business of $2–5,000 — few if any employees.
5		Value or equity $500–2,000 — no employees.
6		Less than $500 equity.
7 (Lowest)		

Source: Adapted by Wendell Bell from W. Lloyd Warner, Marchia Meeker, Kenneth Eells, *Social Class in America*, Chicago: Science Research Associates, Inc., 1949, pp. 140–141, and Carson McGuire, "Social Status, Peer Status, and Social Mobility," a mimeographed memorandum for research workers based upon procedures used in studies for the Committee on Human Development, University of Chicago, Chicago, Ill., 1948.

Table A4 (Continued)

Occupational Rating	White Collar Workers*
1 (Highest)	Executive secretary of status organizations; certified public accountant; editor of reputed newspapers, magazines; executive level of government, Permanent Secretary, Director of Government Department, Undersecretary, Principal Assistant Secretary; Chairman, Parish Council; Member of House of Representatives.
2	Secretary, Parish Council; senior education officer; accountant, insurance, stock and bond, real estate men in reputed firms; columnist, editorial writer, etc.; assistant secretary, organizing secretary of youth organization.
3	Clerk of court, education officer, bank broker's clerk, secretary, senior postal clerk, railroad agent, supervisor in public utilities, parish and civil officials, newspaper reporters, executive officers, etc.
4	Bailiff, cashier, deputy clerk of court, stenographer, bookkeeper, typist, mail clerk, ticket agent; auto, book, clothing, dry goods salesmen, etc.; government clerks, office employees, administrative assistant, clerical officer, prescription pricer — National Insurance Society.
5	Field timekeeper, sugar estate; office boy; drugstore, hardware, grocery, five and ten clerks, etc.; telephone and beauty operator, dressmaker, practical nurse, etc.
6	Note: Actors, authors, musicians, artists, etc. may be rated from "1" to "5" (reputation of their work and degree of acceptance).
7	

* When in doubt about government officers, compare salaries in *The Handbook of Jamaica*.

Table A4 (Continued)

Occupational Rating	Businessmen	Landowners, Farmers, et al.*
1	"Top management" president, manager, executives of corporations, public utilities, banks, et al.	"Gentlemen farmers," landowners not directly supervising operations, the "patrons" of community activities.
2	Assistant, department and office managers or supervisors, managers of large branches, manufacturer's agents.	Landowners, operators, and managers of large properties who have an active urban life.
3	Managers of branch stores and business (no office staff) buyers and salesmen with "connections" (Office and "secretary").	Owners and operators of good mechanized farms with "hired hands."
4		Small landowners and the "forgotten farmer" who owns a "decent place," operators of good leased property employing hired help.
5		Tenants on good farms; owners of farms who just manage to eke out a living, some by "working out"; others by working in plants, supplementing income from crops.
6		Sharecroppers, established farm laborers, subsistence farmers who work out at unskilled jobs, e.g., "cottagers."
7		Migrant worker, unestablished and does not want to be — moves with the seasons, "unemployed — no occupation."

* Sizes of some estates listed in *The Handbook of Jamaica*.

Table A4 (Continued)

Occupational Rating	Service Personnel	Manual Workers
1 (Highest)	Commissioner of Police	
2	Assistant Commissioner of Police, Deputy Commissioner of Police.	
3	Commercial Pilot, Superintendent of Police.	Small contractor who works with his men.
4	Deputy superintendent of police, butcher, tailor, local dry cleaner, railroad and Pullman conductors — ("white collar" men), Assistant superintendent of prison.	Construction, factory or mine foreman; carpenter, electrician, plumber, master mechanic, railroad engineer or trainman, printer, etc.
5	Policeman, barber, gas station operator, butcher's apprentice, bartender, headwaiter, laundry agent, butler.	Apprentice to skilled trades, timekeeper, railroad fireman or brakeman, telephone and telegraph lineman, medium-skilled factory workers, et al.
6	Taxi and truck drivers, baggage men, delivery men, gas station attendant, waitress, chauffeur, etc.	Semi-skilled factory and production workers, warehousemen, janitor, watchman, cook (unless reputed)
7 (Lowest)	Domestic servant (but not butler, housekeeper), busboys, etc., reputed lawbreakers.	Laborer, unskilled miners and mill hands, section hands, migrant workers, scrub women, laundress.

dividual on the basis of the number of reputational nominations he received as powerful regarding the problems of West Kingston. The second component of the Index of Power was a score reflecting the leaders' knowledge of others who were considered to be powerful in dealing with the problems of West Kingston. The first component was assumed to indicate reputation for effective action, or positionally derived potential power, or both. The second factor assumed an association between accurate knowledge of the power of others and effective power for the respondent. It was further assumed that the inclusion of this latter component served to reduce the contribution of position alone to the Index of Power.

The first component of the Index of Power was the score based on reputational nominations. This score was determined by the calculation of the ratio of the number of nominations received by an individual to the possible number of nominations any one individual could have received. The possible number of nominations was determined simply by the number of persons who answered this question:

> Now, I'd like you to tell me the names of the people you think are most important in determining and carrying out policy in relation to the problems of West Kingston.

This listing was completed by 53 respondents. Thus, the number of nominations received by a given leader was divided by 53 and the resulting quotient assigned as a score to be combined with the second component of the index.

Each leader's awareness of the power of others in relation to West Kingston was assessed by comparing his list of names with the combined responses of the total universe. The resulting measure reflects the extent to which a leader agreed with or diverged from the consensus of the remainder of the universe of leaders.

The score was determined in the following manner. The level of agreement was based on the number of "correct" nominations, that is, the number of nominations of persons who were in the top two thirds of the reputational universe. The ratio of the number of "correct" nominations to the number of nominations given was multiplied by the ratio of the number of "correct" to the number of possible "correct" nominations. The resulting measure varies from zero to one. The formula and an example are given below:

$$\frac{\text{``Correct'' nominations}}{\text{Number of nominations made by respondent}} \times \frac{\text{``Correct'' nominations}}{\text{Possible number of ``correct'' nominations}}$$

For example, a respondent who made 41 nominations, 35 of which were persons in the top two-thirds of the universe would be scored as follows:

$$35/41 \times 35/44 = .80$$

This score, as computed above, was then combined with the reputational power score discussed above. The scores of the two components were averaged and the result assigned to the leaders as the Index of Power Scores. The scores were then distributed and dichotomized at the median. Those persons above the median were classified as having high scores on the Index of Power, and those below the median were the less powerful leaders.

The Index of Knowledge. This index is a measure of the leaders' knowledge concerning the discontents and complaints of the people of West Kingston. The leaders were asked:

> What specific discontents and complaints are fairly widespread among the people of West Kingston?

The same information was collected in the sample survey in West Kingston and provided a basis for judging the accuracy and completeness of the responses of the leaders.

The index was based therefore on a simple comparison of the responses of the leaders with the frequency of their occurrence among the residents of the sample area. The responses of the lower-class persons were tabulated, and the marginal percentage for each category of complaint was used as the score given to the leaders who mentioned the categories. For example, 29 per cent of the lower-class sample mentioned lack of water as a major complaint. Each leader who mentioned lack of water as a complaint was given a score of .29. This procedure was followed for each complaint. The total scores assigned to each leader were then distributed and the distribution examined. Heretofore in situations of this sort, the distributions have been arbitrarily cut at the median, primarily because there was no indication that one should do otherwise. It was not so in this case. This distribution was grouped in such a manner that dichotomizing at the median would have resulted in the combination of radically divergent scores. Thus, the cutting point was made above the median at a break in the distribution where the scores classified as high and low were more homogeneous within categories and less between categories. By this means, 63 per cent of the leaders were classified as most knowledgeable.

In those few cases where data were not available for an individual leader, the classification was made on the basis of statements made by the respondent in the interview which indicated that he "didn't know much about the area or the people because he hadn't been down there lately," or some such comment. These classifications were checked against my own personal knowledge of the leader's activity, gained in "participation" with many of them, and observation of them in their work as it related to West Kingston.

APPENDIX 3 Interview Schedule – Jamaican Leaders

1. Considering all the people of Jamaica, from 1938 to the present, in what year do you think they were best off — in 1938, today, or some year in between?
   (IF TODAY) In what ways do you think they are better off today than in earlier years?
   (IF 1938) In what ways were they better off in 1938 than in more recent years?
   (IF SOME YEAR IN BETWEEN) In what ways were they better off in _____ than they were in 1938?
   In what ways were they better off in _____ than they are today?
2. Now, I'd like you to speculate about the future. Generally, do you think the people of Jamaica will be better off, about the same, or worse off after independence (that is, in the future)?
   In what ways do you think they will be better/worse off?
3. Do you think that independence *itself* will make any difference?
   (IF YES) What difference will it make?
   (IF NO) Why do you think that independence will make no difference?

TRANSITION STATEMENT:

In order to focus my interests and delimit the scope of my study, I'm concentrating on an area which seems to be a source of much concern and controversy, that is West Kingston. I'd like to ask you about the area, its people and their problems, and the problems they create for Jamaica.
4. With particular reference to that area do you expect any significant changes to take place after independence (that is, in the future)?

What changes do you expect?
Why?
5. Again, with particular reference to the Western area, what would you say are the most important problems that Jamaican society faces?
Which of these would you say is most important?
Which is least important?
(IF RESPONDENT REFUSES TO CHOOSE ONE AS MOST IMPORTANT)
Can you give me some idea how you see these problems as inter-related?
What would you personally propose as a solution to that problem? (MOST IMPORTANT)
6. Now, I'd like you to tell me the names of the people you think are most important in determining and carrying out policy in relation to the problems of Western Kingston.
7. What specific discontents or complaints are fairly widespread among the people of West Kingston?
8. What organizations or persons speak for the people of West Kingston, that is that express their discontents and complaints to someone who might be able to remedy the situation?
What persons or groups are these?
In your opinion, are these persons or groups effectively expressing the discontents and complaints of the people, and speaking in their interest?
(IF NO) Why do you think they are ineffective?
9. What is actually being done in an attempt to satisfy these complaints and remedy these discontents?
What persons or groups are responsible for that?
Would you say these actions are effective?
(IF NO) Why are they ineffective?
10. Now, I'd like to change the subject a bit. What would you say the middle- and upper-class people think of the people of West Kingston?
How widespread would you say this attitude is?
11. What would you say the people of West Kingston think of the middle- and upper-class people of Jamaica?
12. Do you think it is advisable that any barriers to full interaction of people in Jamaica should be broken down, or are there some status differences which you feel should be maintained?
(IF REDUCE) What kinds of barriers or differences should be reduced?
Are there any you think should be maintained?

(IF MAINTAIN) What kinds of barriers or differences should be maintained?
Are there any you think should be reduced or removed?
14. A few people have told me that some form of civil disorder or violent outbreak is likely to arise out of West Kingston. Do you think it is likely?
15. Some people say that rapid economic development in a relatively poor country like Jamaica is impossible to maintain under a democratic form of government. They argue that democracy does not allow the economically necessary decisions to be made because they are unpopular with the mass of the voters. In general, what is your opinion of this?

Name Index

Adorno, T. W., 73n
Allport, Gordon W., 10
Almond, Gabriel, 58n
Aristotle, 3
Aron, Raymond, 10
Ashenheim, N. N., 100
Augier, F. R., 14n, 39n
Augustine, 3
Ayearst, Morley, 14n

Baillie, John, 3n
Barber, Bernard, 105n
Barringer, Herbert R., 30n
Beard, Charles A., 12
Bell, Wendell, 8, 11, 30, 31, 61n, 67, 69, 70, 72, 73, 74, 76, 77, 81n, 125, 130
Blanksten, George, 30n
Blanshard, Paul, 29
Bock, Kenneth E., 3n
Boulding, Kenneth, 88n, 114
Bradley, C. Paul, 16n
Brinton, Crane, 7n
Broom, Leonard, 31n
Buchanan, William, 10n
Bury, J. B., 2, 3n, 12, 66n, 75
Bustamante, William Alexander, 17, 18, 19, 116

Cantril, Hadley, 7, 10n, 49t, 52, 53, 54, 55
Carr, Edward Hallett, 58, 60, 61
Castro, Fidel, 53, 54
Coleman, James S., 77, 78n
Condorcet, de, M., 66, 75
Conrad, Herbert S., 9n
Cumper, G. E., 28, 29, 33, 119n
Curtin, Phillip D., 14n

Dahl, Robert A., 123n

D'Antonio, William V., 123n
Deutsch, Karl, 29n, 109n
Duke, James T., 26n, 27n, 69, 70
Duzy, E. Stanislaus, 3n, 4n

Edwards, Allen, 59n
Eells, Kenneth, 62n, 130n, 134n
Ellis, Robert A, 121n
Erickson, Eugene C., 123n
Erlich, Howard J., 123n
Eulau, Heinz, 9n, 11, 88n
Eyre, Edward John, 98

Feldman, Arnold, 45, 48, 49t, 50
Foltz, William J., 29n
Fontenelle, de, B., 66, 75
Foskett, John M., 82n
Francis, O. C., 25n
Franck, Kate, 9n
Free, Lloyd A., 7n, 49t, 50, 52n, 65

Gardner, W. F., 14n
Garvey, Marcus, 19
Gibbon, Edward, 58
Ginsberg, Morris, 4n
Glass, Ruth, 34n, 102n
Glazer, Nathan, 110n
Gordon, S. C., 14
Gouldner, Alvin W., 110n
Guttman, Louis, 58n, 59

Hall, Douglas, 14n
Heilbroner, Robert L., 5, 6, 7, 8n, 117
Helleiner, K. F., 5n
Henderson, A. M., 79n
Henriques, Fernando, 73n, 103
Henry, Claudius V., 39
Hildebrand, George H., 3n
Hill, Ken, 16

Name Index

Hill, Richard J., 69n, 81n
Hoetink, H., 35
Hoffer, Eric, 111n
Hohle, Raymond, 82n
Horowitz, Irving Louis, 9
Hughes, Marjorie, 99n
Hyman, Herbert, 96n

Jacobs, H. P., 16
Jahoda, Gustav, 103n
Johnson, Millard, 18
Jouvenel, de, Bertrand, 12

Kaplan, Abraham, 81n
Kluckhohn, Florence Rockwood, 12

Lasswell, Harold D., 9n, 11, 81n
Leroux, P., 66, 75
Lewis, Oscar, 89n
Lightbourne, Robert, 20

Mack, Raymond W., 30n
Manley, Norman Washington, 17, 18, 19, 20, 116
Marcus, John T., 4n
Marx, Karl, 10
Matthews, Donald R., 105n
Maunder, W. F., 32
Mazlish, Bruce, 2n, 5, 58n
McGuire, Carson, 62n, 130n, 134n
Meeker, Marchia, 62n, 130n, 134n
Merton, Robert K., 10, 112n
Mills, C. Wright, 79, 87
Mirin, Linda, 55, 109n, 110n
Moore, Wilbert E., 10, 11, 12
Moskos, Charles C., Jr., 30n, 31, 67, 68, 69, 73, 76, 77, 80n, 125
Myrdal, Gunnar, 9

Naipaul, V. S., 34n, 89n
Nehnevajsa, Jiri, 11
Nettleford, Rex, 39n
Norris, Katrin, 39n, 71n, 101n

Oxaal, Ivar, 8n, 11

Parry, J. H., 14n, 98n
Parsons, Talcott, 66, 79n

Phelps, O. W., 16n
Plato, 3
Polak, Frederik L., 10, 11, 38
Polsby, Nelson W., 123n
Prothro, James W., 105n
Pye, Lucian W., 113

Reckord, M., 14n
Richards, A. F., 17
Riesman, David, 110n
Roberts, George W., 26n
Rousseau, J. J., 66, 75
Rubin, Vera, 71n

Sanford, R. Nevitt, 9
Sangster, Donald B., 19, 20, 21
Selassie, Haile, 39
Shearer, Hugh L., 20, 21
Sherif, Carolyn, 67n
Sherif, Muzafer, 67n
Sherlock, P. M., 14n, 98
Shevky, Eshref, 30n
Simey, T. S., 33
Simpson, George Eaton, 119n
Smith, Adam, 6
Smith, M. G., 27n, 29, 39n, 71, 100n, 121
Spengler, Oswald, 12
Stinchcombe, Arthur L., 55, 109n, 110n
Stouffer, S. A., 58n, 59n
Strodtbeck, Fred L., 12

Teggart, Frederick J., 3n
Thomas, W. I., 12
Trujillo, Raphael, 53
Tumin, Melvin, 45, 48, 49t, 50
Tuveson, Ernest Lee, 4n

Voltaire, F. M., 66, 75

Warner, W. Lloyd, 62n, 130, 134n
Weber, Max, 79n
Wilson, David A., 29, 31n
Wilson, Godfrey, 30n
Wilson, Monica, 30n
Wolfinger, Raymond, 123
Woods, Erville Bartlett, 58n
Wright, Charles R., 81n

Subject Index

Age (of leaders), and belief in hostility of masses, 104
   and belief in progress, 63–64, 73, 83
   and egalitarianism, 72–73
   and knowledge, 91, 93
   and power, 82–83
   distribution, 124

Civil disobedience, 16–17
   fear of, 37–40, 57, 98–101, 111
   Marxism, 101
   Morant Bay Rebellion, 14, 15, 98
   Unemployed Workers' Council, 111
   See also: Ras Tafarians
Color, *see* Race

Decision-making, 8–11
   and power, 81

Economy (Jamaican), 15, 16, 21–26, 32, 40–41, 42, 43, 115
Education, 29, 30, 41, 44, 77
   and belief in hostility of masses, 104
   and belief in progress, 63
   and egalitarianism, 70, 72, 73, 76
   and knowledge, 91–92, 93
   and power, 83, 85–86
Egalitarianism
   and belief in hostility of masses, 105, 107–108
   and belief in progress, 66–67, 75–78, 113–114
   and knowledge, 94–97
   and power, 86
   defined, 66
   trend toward equality, 30–32, 61, 76

   See also: Leaders; Race; Social class
Emigration, 25, 43
Employment, 24–25, 32, 33, 115

Foreign affairs, attitudes toward, 17, 20, 30, 77

Hostility of the masses, 98–112, 121
   myth of, and belief in progress, 104
   and egalitarianism, 105, 107–108
   and knowledge, 106–107
   and power, 104–105

Images of the future
   and social change, 8–12, 41, 43
   as Index of Belief in Progress, 4–5, 57–65
   defined, 38
   differences in, 45–46
   egalitarianism, 76
   favorable, 7, 36–42
   unfavorable, 42–45
Inclusiveness (social), 30–32, 61, 77, 87
Income,
   color and, 28–30
   See also: Economy
Independence,
   and equality, 67, 76–77
   attitudes toward, 37–38, 41, 43–45, 46, 47, 55, 57, 110
   political background of, 42, 99–100, 118
Index, construction of, 130–137
   of Belief in Progress, 57–65
   of Egalitarianism, 67–78
   of Knowledge, 89–90, 136–137

of Political Mobilization, 109–110
of Power, 81–82, 130, 135–136
Industrial development, See Economy
Industrial Development Corporation, 32

Jamaica,
  description, 14
  government in, 15, 17–21, 118
  history of, 14–17
  population, 26–30
    See also: Economy; Nationalism
Jamaica Labour Party, See Political Parties
Jamaica Social Welfare Commission, 64, 65, 75, 84, 92, 125, 126

Kingston-St. Andrew Corporation (KSAC), 64, 93
Knowledge,
  and belief in hostility of masses, 106–108
  and belief in progress, 93–97
  and egalitarianism, 94–97
  and power, 95–97
  defined, 89
  Index of Knowledge, 88, 89–90, 95, 107, 108, 136–137

Labor unions, 16–17, 18, 44
Land distribution, 25, 32–33
Leaders, political, 16–21
  and belief in hostility of masses, 101–112
  and egalitarianism, 68–69, 71–78, 113–114
  and knowledge, 88–97
  and power, 79–87, 114
  attitudes toward, 44–45, 113–114
  defined, 36, 122
  elite positions, 125
  interview schedule, 138–140
  social characteristics, 124
    See also: Social class and leaders
Leaders (religious), 64, 74, 84, 86, 92, 125
Lower class, 27, 32, 33
  and belief in progress, 36, 45–47, 108, 109–110

and independence, 45–46
and political mobilization, 108–109
attitudes of, 39, 45, 48, 50, 54, 55, 56, 98–112
attitudes toward, 34–35, 38, 43, 45, 55–56, 70–71, 89–90, 99, 100
  See also: Knowledge
hostility in, 99–112, 121
social characteristics of, 127–128

Methodology,
  data collection, 118–120, 125
  study design, 121–140
Middle class, 34
  and economy, 24
  attitudes of, 34–35, 89, 99

Nationalism, 16, 17, 31, 41
  African nationalists, 19, 31
  egalitarianism and, 76–77
    See also: Independence

Occupation,
  and belief in hostility of masses, 104
  and belief in progress, 62–63
  and color, 27–28
  and egalitarianism, 72, 73–74, 75, 76
  and knowledge, 91
  and power, 83, 84
  distribution by, 27–28, 124, 125
  rating of, 130–134
  type of elite position and attitudes, 64–65, 74, 84–85, 86, 92

Peoples' National Party, see Political parties
Political development, 15, 17–21, 42, 43, 118, 120
  See also: Political parties
Political mobilization,
  defined, 108–109
  Index of Political Mobilization, 109–110
Political Parties,
  Bustamante Industrial Trade Union (BITU), 17, 18, 20
  Democratic Labour Party, 18, 19
  Jamaica Labour Party (JLP), 18,

19, 20–21, 28, 62, 72, 73, 74, 76, 82, 83, 84, 91, 92, 93, 118, 124–128
National Workers' Union, 18
of leaders and belief in hostility of masses, 104
and belief in progress, 62–65
and egalitarianism, 70, 72, 73, 76
and knowledge, 91
and power, 82–83, 84
Peoples' National Party (PNP), 17, 18, 19, 20–21, 62, 63, 64, 65, 67, 72, 73, 74, 75, 76, 82, 83, 84, 91, 104, 116, 124, 128
Peoples' Political Party, 18
Trade Union Congress, 18
Power (of leaders),
and belief in hostility of masses, 105–106, 107–108
and belief in progress, 85–86
and egalitarianism, 86, 114–115
and knowledge, 96
defined, 81
Index of Power, 81–82, 130, 135–136
Progress,
and belief in hostility of masses, 104
and lower class, 109–112
attitudes toward, 38, 64
belief in, 6, 9, 13, 14, 116
equality and, 66–78, 86, 113–114
idea of, 2–8
Index of Belief in Progress, 57–65
power and, 85–87, 114
See also: Leaders, political

Race (color), 16, 18–19, 26, 27, 28, 29, 39, 120, 124
and belief in progress, 62–63
and equality, 70–71, 72, 73, 75, 76
and knowledge, 91, 92
and power, 83, 84
Ras Tafarians, 39, 98, 111
Religion (of leaders), 124
and belief in progress, 62–63
and egalitarianism, 72, 74, 75, 76
and knowledge, 91, 92, 93–94
and power, 83, 84, 86
See also: Leaders, religious

Slavery, 14, 15, 102
Social change, 14, 30–35, 37, 87
and images of the future, 8–12, 40–41, 43, 60–61
cross-national comparisons, 48–56
evaluation of, 46, 47–48, 61
resistance to, 9
Social class, and attitudes, 45, 48, 50
and belief in progress, 62
and leaders, 61–65
Social development, 42, 49–50
Social mobility, 29
and images of the future, 45
and race, 71
Social structure, 26–32

Unemployment, *see* Employment
Upper class, 27
attitudes of, 34–35, 99
Urbanization, problems of, 25, 30, 32–35, 45, 119

West Indies Federation, 18, 118